Sole Trader

The holistic therapy business handbook

Jane Sheehan

www.footreading.com
www.findafootreader.com

Also by the same author:
Let's Read Our Feet!
The Foot Reading Coach

Sole Trader: The Holistic Therapy Business Handbook
by Jane Sheehan
First Edition 2009

Copyright 2009 © Jane Sheehan

Published by Jane Sheehan
Manor Beeches,
Manor Gardens,
Maids Moreton,
Buckinghamshire,
MK18 1QA,
England
+44 (0) 7739 802175
www.footreading.com
www.findafootreader.com

Some names used in the examples in this book have been changed to protect the identity of those individuals.

A CIP catalogue record for this book is available from the British Library.

ISBN 978-0-9550593-2-2

Design by Nicki Averill Design and Illustration

Contents

Important note

All the legal and financial information recorded in this book relates to English jurisdiction and was correct at the time of going to press. Websites are given for the various governing bodies so that you can check the latest information.

If you are outside England, you will need to contact the relevant authorities in your country for relevant legal and financial advice and guidance.

This publication is designed to provide accurate and authoritative information in regard to the subject matter covered. It is sold with the understanding that the publisher is not engaged in rendering legal, accounting or other professional services. If legal advice or other expert assistance is required, the services of a competent professional person should be sought.

Making the leap

Making the leap!

"You are living as if destined to live forever…you act like mortals in all that you fear, but immortals in all that you desire" Seneca

I remember the fear and trepidation I felt before I ditched my day job to start a new life as a reflexologist and foot reader. Know that you are not the only person to have felt this fear, nor will you be the last. Now, when I talk to my students who are about to embark on just such a journey, I smile to myself as I remember being in their shoes. I know that no amount of words is going to make it right. It's a leap of faith and you only really understand it when you take the leap and experience it for yourself.

How did I take that leap?

I learned reflexology at the Chiltern School of Reflexology in Gerrards Cross, passing my exams in 1999. I then started up my reflexology practice, whilst holding down a day job. I'd spend all day in the office and then most evenings and weekends treating clients. When I added foot reading to my practice the demand got even greater. I became busier and busier and was in danger of burning out! It got to the stage where something had to give. After a lot of soul-searching, I realised that I did not want to give up the therapies, so I knew I would have to give up my day job. For me, this was a seriously daunting prospect. I'd never been in debt, and I'd only ever known salaried employment.

To help me get used to the idea and to prepare mentally and physically, I wrote down my plans on paper, and gave myself measurable goals and a time-frame by which to have carried them out. On a separate sheet of paper, I wrote down my fears. Then I reviewed each item on that list and wrote next to the fear one thing that I could do to allay that fear.

Around this time, I had two quotes to inspire me. The first, which I kept on my kitchen table where I did all my planning, was a quote from Johann Wolfgang Von Goethe:

"Whatever you can do or dream you can, begin it. Boldness has genius, magic and power in it. Begin it now."

The other (from an EVeRYDaY ANGeLS Art scroll), I stuck on the top of my computer screen at my day job. It said

"Here and now are the only moments that exist"

I'd stare at it day in and day out and wonder "If these are the only moments that exist, what am I doing spending them here?" It wasn't that I didn't like my job. I just knew that I wanted more.

In November 2004, I had everything in place and made a commitment to myself that at the end of February 2005 I would hand in my notice, so that by the end of March 2005 I would be starting the first day of the rest of my life self-employed. I didn't tell anyone of my decision. I decided to try it on for size.

From that point forward, every time I got a new client, I was elated. I felt euphoric. This is going to work! Then I'd get a cancellation and I'd plunge into the pits of despair. What would this be like if it was my only source of income?

The thing is, the longer time went on, the more used to the highs and lows I became, and the more excited I found myself. So by the time February arrived, I handed in my notice early! It was a very emotional day. I feel, looking back, that I am a very different person than I was when I started. I've learned many things through trial and error and I wish that this book had existed when I started out.

The first day of my new working life, I appeared on ITV's "This Morning" with Lorraine Kelly and Tris Payne. I saw this as auspicious. Talk about starting as you mean to go on!

There are many different reasons why people start up their own businesses and how they make the leap from salaried to self-employment. Asking around at a business network event, here are some of the stories I heard:

"I was working for a reseller of computers selling to end users but the company shut their doors to the end-user market and started to sell only to wholesalers. I wasn't allowed to direct my selling efforts to the end users. So all these former customers were left with no supplier yet still had a demand for the product. To me, that looked like a good opportunity. I decided to set-up doing exactly the same job I'd been doing for my employers, purchasing from the same suppliers I'd always done and knowing the prices that my employers could purchase at, I was in a very good negotiating position. I was able to scoop up all my old clients. So I ended up making four times as much money as when I was employed. I did it for ten years, but as the computer market got saturated I saw my margins reduce from 30% to 10%. It wasn't a good position to be in as, if there was a bad debt, it could wipe out my profit. So after ten years I incorporated, then sold the business. As part of the deal I worked two days a week for the new owner! Then he sold the business and the new buyer wanted me to work full time. I said either I can work two days a week, or you can buy me out. They decided to buy me out and so I had a nice lump sum to start up my jewellery business."
Liz Coulter, www.splashoutjewellery.co.uk

Note: You can sometimes make more money selling a business than running one.

"I was working part time for Laura Ashley and was on £5 per hour, we had to sell account cards to customers and for this were rewarded with the princely sum of £1 (yes, this is not a typo!) for each card sold. My boss was 18 years old and fresh out of college, she had no life experience or people skills and was very sales driven. I enjoyed the job because customers starting asked for me personally, to dress them for Ascot or weddings but standing on my feet all day in an un-air conditioned fitting room, I started to ask myself "what am I doing here?"

I was also running a local wedding dress shop on a Friday and was on £4.75 an hour, and for each wedding dress I sold I got £5 (but not when I worked on a Saturday!) and £2.50 for every evening gown I hired out. I earned more in "commission" than I did in wages but saw red when I had to ask for a rise of 25 pence an hour. My boss, who was bad tempered beyond belief and "sizeist" (she refused to stock dresses over a size 14) said I was the best sales person she had ever employed yet when I left to set up my own business and she wanted me to help out in an emergency one Saturday and I asked for £10 an hour, (bearing in mind, I was earning £20 an hour when I first set my business up) she lost her temper, tore up all my leaflets, told me I was greedy and completely ignored me in the street.   This proved that I had done absolutely the right thing.

All my work colleagues, friends and family said I must go for it and I did. I started off doing colour analysis on friends to build up my portfolio and within nine months, I had broken even. I did not have a business plan and had a very "suck it and see" approach. Five years on, I am fully booked 6-8 weeks in advance

and am really proud that I have managed to build up a very successful little business with a high media profile locally but firstly still be a Mum to my boys and be able to be there for sports days, school plays, illnesses and be able to meet them at the school gate every day. It is possible to be both a good mother and a successful businesswoman. I absolutely love what I do and there is no turning back!!"
Nancy Stevens, www.alteredimagemk.co.uk

"I was very unhappy at work and being bullied by a colleague. Worse – I'm not the sort of person you'd associate with being bullied either. It really knocked my confidence. My husband told me to resign, so I did. I had a bit of money put away. I fell into website design whilst looking for other work!"
Fiona Storey, www.fionastoreydesign.co.uk

Why bother building a business?

When you start your own business, you're going to have to get used to working longer hours, taking risks, losing your job security, facing rising costs of living and (initially at least) having no pension. Why would you even bother?

Well, that's just one way of looking at it. For me, having my own business means

- being paid to have fun and do what I love
- having the potential to earn more money than when I was employed by someone else
- having freedom to travel and meet interesting people
- structuring my working life how I want to; for example
  - I have long lie-ins and work until late
  - I choose when and where I will work
- pencilling in playtime to suit me
- focusing on creating a passive income
- living below my means
- spending time, energy and money in ways leading to wealth, experience and learning
- having financial independence. I rise or fall through my own efforts.
- enjoying recognition for my efforts

Ideas for your business

How do you know if the moneymaking idea you have is worth pursuing? There's not much point in going into business if you aren't going to at least break even!

- Does the idea fit your business passion? Will it be fun for you?
- Does it add massive value and will it be profitable?
- Will your idea allow you to increase your potential gains even if you have to borrow money?
- Will your idea give you a strategic advantage over your competition?
- Can it be implemented quickly?
- Will it teach you specific skills to help your business in the long run?
- Does the return on investment and time inspire you?

Don't be put off

When I started writing this book, I told a friend that I was planning to write about starting up and running a holistic therapy business and her husband piped up "Aren't there already lots of books about business?"

And therein lies your first lesson about starting your own business. People may inadvertently pour cold water on your ideas before you've even had a chance to put them into action.

However, if you're that easily put off then maybe starting your own business is not for you! It's going to take time, money, perseverance, passion, commitment, learning and action. Reading about it is not a substitute for actually putting it into action!

Is he right? Are there lots of books about starting a business? Yes. But that's a bit like saying "there are loads of shoe shops, why would you open another one?" Would you visit a new shoe shop? I know I would.

So why am I writing this book? I teach foot reading and the most frequently asked questions that I get from my students are about:
■ How can I set up in business?
■ How can I make the leap from regular paid employment to being self-employed?
■ What should I charge?
■ How can I get more clients?

Most people who start their own business, don't start it because they're passionate about business. Far from it. They start it because they've got an interest or hobby about which they are passionate and think it might be fun to get paid to do it for a living. So when they're coming from that starting point, a typical business book might not be as appropriate for them.

I'm writing this book so that you can follow your passion for holistic therapies and translate them into a viable business, without putting you off with lots of business-speak, and hopefully demystifying some of the business dark arts such as marketing, PR and book-keeping!

Goals preparation and timing

Goals, preparation and timing

When you set your own personal goals, it's usually planned in January and often fuelled by alcohol! How mad is that?! I hope that you're not going to do the same for your business goals.

When you get in your car to set off on a journey, you know your starting point and you also know your destination. You then have different route options which you plot. It's no different when you're starting your business. You still need an idea of where you're heading and how you'll know when you get there.

When you set out your goals for your business, you need to make sure that they don't clash with your own personal goals.

Work out your end goals, and then work out how you can break the plan down into smaller milestones. If you can break your goals down into monthly or three monthly intervals with a review date for analysing how on track you are, then you will eventually reach your goals. Better still, get a friend to agree to review the goals with you on that date. There's nothing like having to report to someone else to keep you on track!

It's worth writing down both your personal goals and your business goals. The clearer you can be with your vision, the easier it will be for you to spot synchronistic opportunities along the way.

Don't ignore your fears. Deal with them. Action can cure fear.

I gave a foot reading for a lady in Australia who wanted to start her own business but was very scared and talking herself out of it.

I got her to write down each fear on the left hand side of a piece of paper. As she wrote each fear, you could see her visibly calm down. When problems are allowed to whirl around in your head, they can take on larger-than-life proportions and the issues seem much bigger than they really are. In writing down the fears, she realised that they were not half as big as they had seemed.

Then I asked her to write down a possible action to combat each fear. Soon she was writing a whole list of actions and felt much more in control.

Action:

- ☑ Write down what you want to do. Be very clear, specific and make it measurable.
- ☑ Write down your fears about what you want to do.
- ☑ For each fear, write down all your ideas that could help to minimise those issues.
- ☑ Put those ideas into action.
- ☑ Set up a review date.

SWOT analysis

When I worked in PR and we would help a start-up company, we used to conduct a one day off-site workshop where we'd brainstorm with the company to create a SWOT analysis. (SWOT stands for Strengths, Weaknesses, Opportunities and Threats.) Don't worry, it's not difficult. Strengths and weaknessnes are internal to your business and opportunities, and threats are external to your business. You create four squares like so:

Strengths	Weaknesses
Training	Paper-based database
Networking	Income reliant on time
Opportunities	Threats
National spend on holistic therapies forecast to increase	Legislation
	Recession

In the Strengths column, you put all the characteristics that make you special and set you apart from the competition.

In the Weaknesses column you put all the things you need to overcome or that your competitors could take advantage of.

In the Opportunities column you put anything you can do that might benefit your business either now or in the future.

In the Threats column you put anything that can harm your business.

I remember for one company, when working with them on the "Threats" column, we asked them what they would do if their funding dried up. They were so confident that it would never happen, they refused to examine the threat. A year later, the person funding them withdrew his support due to business concerns elsewhere. If it were your business, wouldn't you have wanted to explore the options and considered a strategy well before it ever happened?

Action:

☑ What are you waiting for? Write your own SWOT analysis out now.

Strengths	Weaknesses
Opportunities	Threats

☑ Use your answers to help you with your marketing and your business strategy.

Goals

Now you've worked out your strengths, weaknesses, opportunities and threats, it's time to sort out your goals.

When you look at your goals, I'm not just talking about your business goals. You can't see them in isolation. One of the biggest mistakes people make is focusing too much in one area of their life whilst all the rest of it goes wrong! There are enough stories of "successful" business people out there who've left a trail of failed marriages and estranged children because of their commitment to their business. Learn from their mistakes.

A simple economic principle is that of "opportunity cost". If I spend my time and energy doing project A, then I cannot spend my time and energy doing project B. I have to make a choice and when looking at it through an economist's eyes, the choice would be to choose the project that uses the resources most efficiently for the maximum results. As a holistic therapist, the motivations are not all about money. They may be about helping others, about finding balance, about having an amazing experience etc. So, when you set your goals, you need to be very clear about what those choices are and what the opportunity cost of what you are doing is and how you will measure the "cost" because it doesn't necessarily have to be about the monetary value (although you won't have much of a business if you don't keep an eye on a monetary target that will at least let you break even).

Action:

Write down your goals, not forgetting to include your personal as well as your business goals. To get you started, you can get a free work/life balance planner from www.your-business-matters.com/work_life_balance_planner.htm

On it, you are given the following list of categories. Taking each category in turn, you are asked to score where you are on a scale of 1 to 10 with 10 being perfect and zero meaning the worst.

- Fun and recreation
- Personal growth
- Relationship
- Home
- Health
- Energy
- Money
- Friends and Family
- Attitude
- Career/business

Then you reflect and write down key actions to improve your satisfaction with each area. The idea is that you implement the key actions and review your score at monthly intervals. Perhaps you'd like to choose a friend to review with you at set intervals whether you've implemented key actions. If you know there's someone checking up on you, you're more likely to take action!

Remember to make your goals specific, measurable, achievable and with a timescale for review.

Action:
☑ Set your business goals
☑ Set your personal goals

Timing

"It's not that we have a short time to live, but that we waste a lot of it" Seneca

There are annual quiet times for most therapy businesses. Where I live, these are Christmas and August. If I lived by the seaside I'm sure they would be at different times! It would make no sense to try to start a business during those quiet periods. Through asking other therapists in your area, find out when the quiet times are in your proposed business area and plan to take your own holidays then or to work on your business strategy.

Greg's business is seasonal. In the low season he only works at weekends. In the high season he works from 7am to 11pm, seven days a week. Yet for the whole of winter, he does not have any work at all. He's learned to spend winter in India where he can live much more cheaply, making his savings go a lot further, and where he can really recharge his energies, ready for starting back in the spring.

Remember – even when the money isn't coming in, you can still offer a treatment in exchange for another service. You will need to invoice in the usual way and show it in your accounts in the usual way, but show that you accepted a service of equivalent value in lieu of payment. If you're VAT registered then you will still have to deal with the VAT payment in the usual way.

Action:

Anticipate your quiet times and plan to use them effectively, either to rest, plan your strategies or to learn new skills.

Preparation

What kind of preparation do you need to make in order to start your business?

- ☐ Have a clear vision.
- ☐ Know your market, including your potential customers and your competition.
- ☐ Have savings. Calculate how long you could survive comfortably if no money were coming in.
- ☐ Write a business plan as a roadmap for your business.
- ☐ Decide on the legal/tax status of your proposed business.
- ☐ Write a forecast to help you budget.
- ☐ Improve your business skills.
- ☐ Build a team (not necessarily paid) who can give you sound business advice.
- ☐ Build a support network.
- ☐ Write your business guarantees.
- ☐ Understand budgeting and cash flow forecasting (see Money chapter).
- ☐ Set up your accounts templates/spreadsheets
- ☐ Long term, you may need to build a high performing team to manage your business so it can function without you.

> ## Action:
> Start tackling your preparation for each of the above points. Use the following sections to help you clarify your thinking.

Know your market

You're about to give up your salaried work to make the leap into self-employment. On what are you basing your decisions? Do you have a gut-feeling that if you start this business, it will work out? Are you using your intuition? Are you scared whether it will work out or not?

How about putting in a bit of research before you start? Knowing more about the market will help you understand whether your idea is viable. It's not difficult to do and usually someone else has already done it! You can glean a lot of market information through government statistics or from your local reference library or from your trade association. I telephoned the Association of Reflexologists and asked them if they had any statistics about the reflexology market.

- There are 32,000 reflexologists in the UK.
- The average treatment fee in the UK is £25.
- Holistic spending is six billion pounds a year and growing.
- One in five people in the UK uses complementary therapies.
- 90% of the Association of Reflexologists' members are self-employed, working on a part-time basis and the majority practise at least two therapies.

Source: Doreen Baker, Chief Executive of the Association of Reflexologists, December 2008.

You can do your own market research. I read "Anyone can do it: Building Coffee Republic from our kitchen table" by Sahar and Bobby Hashemi. When they were choosing where to site their first coffee shops, they stood outside each of the proposed properties and counted the number of people who walked past the shop to get an idea of the potential market for each property. It's a simple idea, yielding useful, timely, relevant information and only cost them time.

Shut your eyes and imagine that you are sitting on a bench in your local shopping centre. It's a busy Saturday afternoon and you are noticing all the people walking past. Some are Mums with push-chairs and toddlers in tow. Some are groups of teenagers dawdling along. Some are pensioners with tartan trolleys. They've all got money in their pockets and they've all come out to the shopping centre to spend it. How are you going to persuade them that they should spend it with you?.....

- Who are your potential customers?
- Where do they hang out?
- How much are they prepared to spend?
- How often are they prepared to spend?
- What do they like doing and spending?
- When do they seek your type of service?
- What is their motivation to spend on your type of service? What's in it for them?
- What do they like and dislike about similar services to yours?
- What can they experience through your service that they can't get anywhere else?

Knowing the above information will help you know how to reach your potential customers, how to propose the right kind of offer to entice them and how to keep them as customers once you have persuaded them to try your service.

Action:

Research your market. Evaluate what they want. Consider how you can provide what they want, at a price they are willing to pay. Consider whether you can attract enough customers to have a viable business.

Savings

I said earlier in the section on timing that you will experience quiet periods in your business. Because of this, you need to have some savings so that you can survive these quiet periods. Unlike with salaried employment, you won't have the regular monthly pay cheque so you need to set aside money for the quiet times. Expect your income to arrive in peaks and troughs and don't spend it all during the peaks so that you can minimise the disruption of the troughs. Sounds like a no-brainer but you'd be surprised how many people forget this simple principle.

Before you give up your day-job, reduce all your outgoings. Check out Martin Lewis's website **www.moneysavingexpert.com** to get some ideas of how you can lower your bills and maximise your savings. Then set an annual review date to ensure you keep costs to a minimum.

Once you have left your day job, it's still a good idea to put aside a proportion of all your earnings in a savings account in case of any unexpected bills, tax requirements or unexpected illness where you aren't able to work for a while. Get in the habit of setting aside a proportion of your income right from the start. You can always put it back when it's needed, but starting as you mean to go on will create good business habits that will stand you in good stead later.

Make sure you charge enough for your services.

For example, if you took up Reiki and believe that the healing energy that you provide is a gift from God and therefore you feel you cannot charge for that gift – how are you going to satisfy the need to keep a roof over your family's head? Charging for the gift may not be appropriate, but charging for your time can be appropriate.

Set an annual date for reviewing your bank accounts to move them to a higher interest-earning account.

Financially, plan for the worst and hope for the best.

Cash-flow is the lifeblood of your business. Without it you have no business. If you grow your business too quickly, you could find that you've tied all your cash up in stock, with no spare cash for operational needs. Keep an amount in savings to buffer you against such sticky patches. Avoid cash flow problems by chasing revenue when it becomes due and when offering credit terms, keep the timescales short.

Action:

- ☑ Reduce your outgoings
- ☑ Increase your savings
- ☑ Transfer a proportion of everything you earn into a separate account
- ☑ Set an annual date for reviewing your finances and finding better rates

Write a business plan

You'll often get told that you need a business plan. But why? What is it? What does it do? Is it worth the effort of writing one?

Darren Taylor holds the World Record for diving 35 feet into 12 inches of water. His "sport" is shallow diving, which involves leaping from ever-greater heights into a 10 ft by 5ft paddling pool holding just 12 inches of water. He broke his own world record by jumping from a breathtaking 35ft 4in. A conventional dive, head first, would of course be lethal. Darren has been pushing back the limits of his nerve since 1983. He describes the shallow dive as the "mother of all belly flops" and says his secret is "never ever look into the pool". "There is fear. But you mainly make sure you have a good flight plan" he said.

Using Darren Taylor's flight plan as an analogy – your business plan is your flight plan to ensure your business stays on target, stays alive and helps to reduce the fear and helps you to keep your nerve! It's your plan of how you're going to steer your business into profit. In it you will write about what you want to achieve with your business and how you will set about achieving it. Remember to make your goals realistic, measurable and achievable. As it's a business, the usual way to measure it is to set turnover figures, cash-flow figures and, eventually, profit figures.

When you write a business plan for a business that you have not even started yet, most of the figures that you put into the plan will be your best guesses, rather than actual figures. So it's a good idea to keep revisiting your plan after you have started to revise the plan so that it fits the reality of your situation. That way you'll be able to identify any problem areas sooner rather than later.

Avoid being vague. The objective of the plan is to secure results and for results you need to be able to track your progress and to follow up. You need to include specific dates, budgets, milestones, and an idea of who is responsible. Tailor your plan to its real business purpose.

For some useful tips on writing a business plan, you can refer to **http://www.businessplanhelp.co.uk/** or contact your bank as they often have printed guides to help you understand what they expect from a business plan.

As well as using the business plan to help you steer your business, you'll need a business plan if you are applying for finance or credit. Most lenders won't even consider a credit application from a business that doesn't have a comprehensive business plan. Your business plan demonstrates to lenders that you're serious about your new venture and have a viable plan. (Or in a few cases, demonstrates that you don't!)

Business schools will tell you that there are seven main parts to a business plan:

- Summary – where you summarise your entire business plan.

- Business description – where you give background information about the industry and your target market.

- Market strategies – include market research then say exactly how you will reach prospective clients. Focus on what makes your company unique. Include your marketing plan.

- Competitive analysis – Consider potential competitors in your area. Analyse their strengths and weaknesses and then contrast them against what you perceive to be your own. (See section on SWOT analysis.)

- Design and development plan – consider how you'll develop market opportunities to help your business prosper and grow. Have a timetable of objectives that you can use as a way of benchmarking your success, e.g. set a goal for growing your client base by a certain percentage or set a goal for your client retention rate. If you're planning on opening more than one site, then you may want to show the different stages of development and use those to apply for finance at each stage.

- Operations and management plan – outline the day-to-day operations of your business. Are there employees, how is the hierarchy etc.

- Financial factors – If you are a start-up company then you'll need to forecast the success of your business. The idea is to keep your business financially on track, provide a benchmark against which to compare your success and help you to avoid unpleasant surprises. If it's an existing company, how did the company perform last year in terms of profit and loss, budgeting and cash flow and what are the comparative performance indicators this year?

When using a business plan to approach financial institutions, underpromise and overdeliver.

Embarrassing confession time: When I started out in my business, I didn't know anything about business plans. But that doesn't mean to say I didn't write anything down. I just didn't formalise it like this. I had a little notepad that I kept by the side of the bed and each night I'd write down ideas, hopes, dreams, things I was grateful for - that sort of thing. It's something I've always done. I find if you write things out they have a way of happening, even if you're not consciously working on them.

I dug it out when I was writing this book to see what I'd written. On 14 November 04 after I'd been filling my leisure time with my therapy work and just as I was planning to leave my day job, I'd written
- By March 05 conduct monthly seminars with minimum of 10 people at £50+ per head
- Give seminars internationally
- Write book by 14 November 05
- Have 4 reflexology clients a day five days a week for 49 weeks of the year
- In two years time have full financial freedom

So despite not knowing about doing business plans, I really did have a strong idea about what I wanted to do and had made it measurable. As it turned out, I wrote the book well before the target date too!

I recognised very early on in the planning stages of my business that if I wasn't careful, I'd always be paid an hourly rate for my work. That worried me because I recognised that any sickness, or unforeseen mishap would directly affect my earning potential. I knew I had to find a way to shift my business from solely hourly income to creating passive income. Passive income means the money that you earn when you're not even there e.g. earning interest from an investment, earning money from affiliate programmes, selling anything that is automatically renewable or selling consumables that are automatically re-ordered. I feel it is so important that I've included a section about passive income in the chapter about Money.

I also recognised that in business you can make more money selling a business than actually running one. But making money is not my sole reason for being in business so that's an idea that doesn't feature in my current business plan.

I've asked around some of my pals about whether they did a business plan and quite a few have openly admitted that they did not write a formal business plan, but they did jot a similar bullet point plan. One of them told me that over 50% of all business start-ups that don't have a business plan fail in the first year and 85% fail in the first five years. So at least put down a little plan of what you want to do even if it's not as formal as the official seven point plan that business schools recommend.

Action:

Write your business plan. Make it measurable and achievable.

Decide upon the legal/tax status of your business

How are you going to structure your business? It can have both legal and practical implications[1]. You'll need to decide between

■ Sole Trader
■ Partnership
■ Limited Liability Company
■ Limited Liability Partnership

Sole Trader

Most of the holistic therapists to whom I've spoken, set up as sole traders almost by default. A massive 71% of all British businesses have no employees according to Department of Trade and Industry figures. The majority of sole trading enterprises are in the service sector. The popularity of this type of business reflects the ease with which you can start sole trading. Registration is straightforward, record keeping is simple and you get to keep all the profits after tax. Mind you, if your business fails, you will have to pay for that failure out of your own pocket.

■ You must pay income tax on any profits your business makes.

■ You need to complete a self-assessment tax return each year, detailing your income and expenses. You also have to keep records of all your income and expenditure (including receipts).

■ You must register as self-employed with HM Revenue and Customs (HMRC). **There is a fine if you fail to register within the first three months of trading.**

---

1   As the law and tax rules are constantly changing, please consult your legal and financial professionals before deciding. The information given here was correct at time of printing and applies to England only.

- You need to register for VAT if your turnover is going to be more than £60,000 a year (this figure was correct at time of going to press, but do check with HMRC - http://www.hmrc.gov.uk/ - for latest figure as it could change). This means you'll charge VAT on all your goods or services and will have to complete and submit a VAT return to HMRC each year.

- You'll be taxed on the profits you make (as this is your income) in the form of National Insurance Contributions (NICs), either Class 2 or Class 4. Contact HMRC for current rates - http://www.hmrc.gov.uk/.

Partnership

A partnership is a business arrangement where 2 or more people (usually up to a maximum of 20) are self-employed and in business together to make a profit. All partners share the business costs, profits and debts – regardless of who incurred the debt or made the profit. Partnerships work well when each partner brings a different skill/area of expertise to the business and the workload is divided up to reflect each of the partners' strengths. That's the official consensus anyway. My personal view is different. Of the few people I know who have entered a partnership, they have all ended in tears. I think that people like the idea (probably because of the shared finance and shared responsibility) but how much better to work for yourself and make your own decisions (and keep all the profit). A partnership is like a marriage – if it goes bad, it can be as messy as a divorce! Knowing this, it's a good idea to choose your partner with as much or even more care than you would when looking for a marriage partner and set out at the beginning the areas of responsibility, how the partnership will be dissolved (just in case!) and consider changes in circumstances. For example, how will the partnership cope with a long-term illness or pregnancy necessitating one of the partners reducing their input?

- Individual partners and the partnership need to complete a self-assessment tax return each year, detailing their income and expenses. They also have to keep records of all income and expenditure.

- Each partner must register as self-employed with HM Revenue & Customs - http://www.hmrc.gov.uk/. **There is a penalty if you fail to register within the first 3 months of trading.**

- The partnership should register for VAT (if its turnover is going to be more than the threshold). This means they'll charge VAT on all goods or services, and will have to complete and submit a VAT return to HMRC each year.

- Partners are taxed on a share of the profits (this is their income) in the form of National Insurance Contributions (NICs), either Class 2 or Class 4. See http://www.hmrc.gov.uk/ for latest rates.

Limited Liability Company

A limited company is one whose shareholders (members or owners) have limited liability to the company's debts. Their liability is restricted to the value of the shares that they own or the guarantees that they sign up to, for example a loan they have guaranteed.

A limited company is a separate legal entity. It can sue and be sued and will continue to exist even if the members or owners die or resign. It can only be folded if it is wound up or struck off the register by Companies House.

In return for these benefits, limited companies are governed by tighter rules and regulations than partnerships or sole traders.

- A registration with Companies House is required and accounts must be filed each year.

- A company must be made up of a minimum of one director and a company secretary.

- Company management decisions must be made by a director or the board of directors.

- A company is required to pay corporation tax and each year to file a return with HM Revenue and Customs.

- All employees and directors have to pay income tax as well as Class 1 National Insurance Contributions.

- Each year a 363s form will be sent to the company (before the anniversary of incorporation). This form must be checked, any changes should be made and then it should be returned to Companies House along with the required monies.

- Should the structure or management of the company change in any way Companies House must be notified, either by a director or company secretary.

- Limited Liability Companies pay Corporation Tax. See http://www.hmrc.gov.uk/ for latest rates.

Limited Liability Partnership

This legal business structure aims to combine the flexibility of a partnership agreement with the benefits of limited liability. The main differences between a Limited Liability Company and an LLP are that the latter is taxed as a partnership rather than as a corporation and that it has more organisational freedom. An LLP's duties in return for the limited liability status are similar to those applying to limited companies.

- File annual accounts and returns at Companies House, facing penalties if late.

- Each year a 363s form will be sent to the company (before the anniversary of incorporation). This form must be checked, any changes should be made then it is returned to Companies House along with the required monies.

- Individual partners and the partnership need to complete a self-assessment tax return each year, detailing income and expenses. You also have to keep records of all your income and expenses.

- Have at least two "designated members" – these members have more responsibilities than other company members and they will be held accountable for failing to fulfil them.
- Notify any changes to members, officers or registered office address.
- Partnership members get taxed based on the share of the profits they receive. They also pay National Insurance Contributions.

"Having had a dad who ran his own business successfully and a brother who ran a business that spectacularly failed, I did set up a limited liability company. I'd advise, don't rush in too quickly. Knowing what I know now, I would have taken longer to set things up and put support networks in place. I did a course which helped to set up that support network of like-minded people. It was really valuable. Looking back I'd advise anyone to take longer than you think you need over the transition from wage-earning to self-employment."
Andrew Newton, Non-Denominational Celebrant
at.newton@btinternet.com   07854358692

Note: At a recent workshop, one of my students reported that as she was in full-time employment, and she wasn't making a profit yet with her part-time business, she didn't see the point of including it on her self-assessment. Apart from the fact that she will be fined for not declaring it, she may be making a financial mistake. There are occasions where the losses you sustain on one business can be off-set against a tax-bill for other employment. If it's your first year of business, you can carry losses forward to set against income that will be made in future years.

Action:

Decide what type of business set-up you will have. Do this in consultation with your chosen accountant or legal advisor.

Naming your business

There are limits on using certain words in your business name. They are set out in the Business Names Act 1985 and the Company and Business Names Regulations Act 1981. For more information visit Companies House website **(http://www.companieshouse.gov. uk/about/gbhtml/gbf3.shtml)** or the National Business Register.

Don't pick a name that is similar to another well known business name as you could face legal action. To be absolutely sure that you can use a name, contact a solicitor to perform the checks or register your name with the National Business Register who will do the checks for you and ensure nobody copies it in the future or passes it off as their own.

If you're going to trade under a name different to your own personal name you must display the name of the owners and an address where documents can be served on all business stationery and at your premises. Design letterheads, business cards and signage accordingly.

Action:

☑ Choose your business name.
☑ Check that it is not contravening any legal Act.
☑ Ensure the owner's name and address are on business stationery and displayed at the business premises

Write a forecast to help you budget

When you think of a business, you think in terms of sales price less costs equals profit. However, that's not enough. In a business, we don't spend the profits, we spend cash. Cash flow is an important factor to consider. That's why you need to get good at forecasting and budgeting.

When you first start your business, your forecast will be your best guess, and then you'll revisit it regularly to compare your best guess with the reality.

Think about where you will find income and where, and on what, you will have to spend to create that income. Then think about how much you would need to pay yourself to keep your head above water. See example opposite.

It's not unusual for the business to be making a loss in the first year. What is important is to know how many months it will take to start making a profit and how that profit can be sustained. That's why it is important to make a forecast and use it as a guide to see from month to month how your business is faring. If you're not hitting targets then you're going to have to seriously review what works and what is not working for your business and address those issues. This will help you to see the early warning signs before you get yourself into horrendous debt spirals.

So now you know the importance of your forecast, you know that you need to make your guesses about costs as accurate as possible and err on the side of caution. Make your financial goals as realistic as possible. Review regularly. Knowledge is power.

I can remember when I first started my business I got totally frustrated when having to forecast because it really did feel like blind guesswork. Of course, that's exactly what it was. It's not until you start actually doing

A forecast could look like this:

Income	Month 1	Month 2	Month 3	Month 4
Treatments	100	200	300	400
Merchandise	50	100	200	400
Etc				
Total incomings	150	300	500	800
Outgoings				
Treatment products	5	10	15	20
Purchase of merchandise (greater discounts on larger quantities)	25	50	75	150
Room hire	300	300	300	300
Travel	150	150	150	150
Bank loan	100	100	100	25
Purchase of equipment	2000	-	-	-
etc				
Total outgoings	2580	610	640	645

Using the above forecast, the profit and loss forecast would look like this

	Month1	Month2	Month3	Month4
Brought forward from previous month		(2430)	(2740)	(2880)
Total incomings	150	300	500	800
Less total outgoings	2580	610	640	645
Monthly Profit or Loss	(2430)	(2740)	(2880)	(2725)

the work that you get a feel for the numbers. Hence, keep reviewing your forecast regularly and adjusting your expectations and efforts accordingly. In your second year, you'll have a track record which you can use as a basis for forming your forecast for the subsequent year.

Action:

Create a best guess forecast for your first year and review the reality on a monthly basis against your forecast.

Improve your business skills

Let's face it, most holistic therapists get into business because they have a passion for helping people, or for what they do, but many don't have the necessary business skills required when they first start out. It's often a case of learning on the job. One thing is for sure – when you have to know how to do something, you learn more attentively! There are lots of places you can turn to for help.

- Who do you know who is already able to do what you need to know? Would they be willing to tell you over a coffee and a cake?
- Contact your local branch of the various business support agencies that were set up to help people just like you. Here's a few:
  - Business Link www.businesslink.gov.uk
  - Federation of Small Businesses www.fsb.org.uk
  - National Federation of Enterprise Agencies www.nfea.com
  - Learn Direct www.learndirect.co.uk
  - Train to Gain www.traintogain.gov.uk

If you know of any other useful sources, why not mention it on the forum at **www.footreading.com** so that others can benefit from your knowledge.

Whilst you are still in salaried employment, you can take advantage of learning as much as you can from the various sections at your current workplace. Each of the staff in those sections can teach you different aspects of a business so that you can grow your knowledge. When you leave the company, keep their phone number in case you want to run an idea past them.

Don't overlook retired people. Not only might they have a wealth of experience and expertise but they also have the time to talk things through with you and research topics (and they might even enjoy being involved).

After you've started to make a profit, allocate 10% of your earnings towards training yourself in the skills you feel you need to progress your business.

In the meantime, turn your car into a university. You can get business books on CD or tape from your local library and if you spend a lot of time travelling to and from places, then you can use that time more efficiently by listening to those CDs in your car to help you to acquire new business skills to assist you with your business. If you're comfortable with technology, you could even download some of the many free talks from the internet.

Action:
Create an action plan to enable you to acquire the business skills you'll need.

Build a support network

Before you make the leap into self-employment, think of all the people you know who have really good business skills. Make a list. Approach each of the people on your list and explain that you're going to start up your own business and would they mind you contacting them from time to time to bounce around some ideas.

You'll be surprised by how helpful people can be when they are talking about a topic in which they're knowledgeable. Think about the last time someone asked you about your field of expertise. Were you reluctant to help or did you share your knowledge freely?

Building a support network is essential. As a business owner you need many diverse skills and I'd be surprised if you had them all. I know I don't. Where I don't, I either find someone who can talk me through it, or I pay for the expertise (or both).

In addition to professional advisors, it's worth setting up a network of people in synergistic businesses to you so that you can cross-fertilise ideas and even share clients.

> A body-worker I know sends clients of his to a chiropractor, and the chiropractor in turn sends people to him for muscle work.

Working on your own can sometimes feel isolating, so the sooner you build your network the better.

If you're not naturally great at networking, you could consider joining a formalised network group. (See section on "Networking".)

Action:
- ☑ Write a list of all the people you know who have expertise in an area that you may need. Arrange to meet them.
- ☑ Write a list of business owners who have synergistic businesses to yours. Meet with them to discuss how you can help each other.
- ☑ Find out about the local business network events in your area. Choose one to visit.

Business guarantees

When you start your business, what is your customer guaranteed if they are going to spend their hard earned cash with you?

Have a think about what you are going to provide to your customer and what you would do for that customer if what they receive is less than the standard that you think they deserve.

Let's face it, sometimes things go wrong. A new customer is hard to win. You have to catch their attention, impress them, and then get them to act differently from how they'd usually act. Any way you can find to encourage their trust in you and your business is worth doing. Plus, any way you can ensure that they understand what you think is acceptable (so that when it falls short of that, they know how you will put things right) is surely a good step to take for any business.

You have the added advantage that by setting out your business guarantees, the customer will act as an early warning system if something happens to go wrong. You are ensuring that they are "brave" enough to give you the valuable feedback that you need in order to put it right in a timely fashion.

For example, when I printed my second book, I used the same printer, but they subcontracted to a different binder. I was horrified to discover that there were occasional copies where there were blank pages on pages 22/23 and pages 27/28. I then found out that some copies had pages falling out. It took some time before the news filtered back to me so that I could remedy the problem. I learned several valuable lessons from this. I put myself in the shoes of the customer (no pun intended) and asked myself how I would feel if I'd just spent good money on a book that was faulty. How would I want it handled?

As a result, I decided to formalise the ideas of what I was prepared to do as a business to put things right and to put a guarantee on my website so that everyone who ordered one of my books would know that I would replace the faulty items.

What I hadn't anticipated was that this simple step would increase my sales. It's something I wish I'd done from day one.

Having a business guarantee justifies a higher price as it takes away the perceived risk. It can increase your conversion rate from prospective customer to customer. It separates you from your competition. It generates more enquiries because it reduces the fear factor. If you make your guarantee quite outrageous it can create a word-of-mouth buzz so it can save you money in reduced marketing costs. (Remember Domino Pizzas who guaranteed delivery within 30 minutes or you get your pizza for free?)

The reason why most people don't give a business guarantee is because they fear that people will claim on it (but only 5% are likely to). When you look at your own business, don't you agree that if something goes wrong you will do everything in your power to put it right? Most customers just want their problem fixed.

Recently I ordered a CD off the internet. It was a company I'd not used before. Imagine the goodwill created between me, the recipient, and the company, when I received the CD as requested, but it was accompanied by the following letter:

Dear Miss Sheehan

Thank you very much for your purchase and I do sincerely hope you enjoy your item.

If there is a problem with your order, please email me before returning an item.

I would be very honoured (and appreciative) if you took the time to leave me a positive rating on <name of website>.

If you were in anyway dissatisfied with our service or the product that you received, please notify me immediately. I will do whatever it takes to make you happy. Your satisfaction is my number 1 Goal.

I strive for 100% customer satisfaction and a 5 Star Feedback Rating. Please don't leave a 4 star (or lower) rating, as that is calculated as a negative by <name of website> and it really hurts my business. If for any reason you do not feel that I deserve a 5 Star Rating, please contact me before leaving any rating. As soon as I receive your rating, I will also rate you as a buyer with 5 Stars.

Thank you again for giving me this opportunity to service your media needs.

Best wishes and kind regards

If your business is concerned with the environment - for example if you're a setting up a recycling business - you'll also need to make sure you comply with the Environmental Information Regulations.

If you want to learn more about how to systemize your business, consult *Instant Systems* by Bradley J Sugars (ISBN 978-0071466707).

Action:

☑ Consider your paperwork and put systems in place.
☑ Consider the requirements of the Data Protection Act.
☑ Consider the legal requirements for the storage of financial data.
☑ Systemise your business processes

Getting business to come to you

Getting business to come to you

I once asked my friend Birdwatcher Martin what is it that would make someone pay you their hard-earned cash. He said "Give 'em what they can't get at home and charge them for it." With hindsight I think he was making a rude joke that completely sailed over my head. But behind jokes there is often a grain of truth.

There are different motivations behind making purchases – the pursuit of happiness, the avoidance of fear, the suppression of inadequacies to name but a few. Analysing the motivations behind why people would choose to pay for your service will help you to know what kind of marketing message you will offer.

When he's not joking, Birdwatcher Martin often talks a lot of good sense. He was teaching me about the finer points of "twitching". Twitchers are very serious birdwatchers who have a list of birds that they'd like to see in their lifetime. They set about systematically trying to tick off each of the birds on their list. Some have more than one list, e.g. a local list, a national list, a migration list etc. He explained that there are different ways to go about birdwatching. You can either

- Stand outdoors and hope that if you stand there long enough, all the birds on your list will come to you (though highly unlikely).
- Or you can find out more about each species and put out their favourite food to attract them (more successful).
- Or his preferred method is to find their preferred habitat and go there (much more chance of finding what he's looking for).
- A fourth option, which I think he may consider "cheating", would be to combine options two and three and achieve an even better score!

■ Serious twitchers have a network where they inform each other of birdwatching opportunities.

The more you think about it, the more you realise that finding customers is a lot like birdwatching.

■ You can just set up your service with an "if I build it, they will come" attitude, a bit like standing in a field hoping to find the right birds.

■ Or you can work out what your potential customers would actually need, want or desire, and set that up as the "bait" to attract them.

■ Or you can actually investigate where your ideal customer would "hang out". What's their natural habitat? Take yourself out to where they are and you've more chance of finding your customers and them finding you.

■ Or you can combine options two and three above and achieve a greater potential client base and even have them come to you.

■ Or you might network with other non-competing therapists.

Birdwatcher Martin took me on a 24 hour bird race where we had to "spot" as many birds as possible in the given time. Within minutes we got into an argument about what constituted an acceptable "tick". We heard the call of a great tit, "teach-er, teach-er, teach-er". He recorded it on his list. I was horrified. "But you didn't see it. That's cheating". He argued, "When your Mum calls you on the phone, you don't have to see her to know that it's her." I learned that by changing the way you do things can improve your success!

When is a customer not a customer? Either when they purchase something and return it (although you give a refund and on paper it looks like you've lost nothing, you've lost the initial postage, time and let's face it, time is money, and unless the item is in pristine condition you'll have to re-sell it at a discount), or when they make a booking and fail to show up or regularly cancel or postpone (you've therefore lost the opportunity to do something more profitable with that time slot). There comes a point when you have to recognise that there are some customers that you can do without. Recognising them and having the courage to say "No" is a learned skill but one that you need to develop rather quickly if you want your business to succeed. Even better would be to pre-determine a policy which will help you to avoid attracting such behaviour in the first place. For example, in the case of cancellations, maybe it would be good to have a clearly defined cancellation policy that the client is made aware of at the time of booking. (See section on "Should you sack a client?")

Action:

- ☑ Who is your ideal customer?
- ☑ How can you reach them?
- ☑ What offer can you give them to entice them to use your services?
- ☑ Set up your cancellation policy

What's your USP?

In marketing circles you'll hear the initials "USP" bandied about a lot. It merely stands for unique selling point. Have a think about you and your proposed business. What is it about you and about your proposed business that is unique? What is the discriminator that sets you apart? Why should a potential customer come to you rather than go to a competitor? When you know the answer to these questions, then that is your USP and by identifying what it is, you will need to make all your potential customers aware of what it is. Why are you so unique that they should be beating a path to your door? Sometimes it's one thing, or sometimes it is a set of things. Remember to drop it in all your conversations about your business, all your leaflets, business cards, and customer-facing messages.

Many reflexologists work part-time only or have more than one therapy that they offer. If you are looking for a Reflexologist and happen to ring Sylvia Ferguson you will hear "You have reached Sylvia Ferguson, specialist in foot reflexology". Immediately you will note that how she describes herself, although clearly a reflexologist, sets her apart from all the other people that you have telephoned. This is her USP. It's also not enough for her to just say so. When you enter her treatment room, you will see row upon row of certificates showing her many areas of training, all relating to different forms of reflexology.

Action:

☑ What is your USP?
☑ How are you going to let your customers know?

Synergistic offerings

Who do you know who offers synergistic services to what you do. What I mean by that is who offers services that may be of benefit to your clients that will not clash but will enhance the service that you offer?

For example, as reflexology is a complementary therapy not an alternative therapy, I have a list of synergistic services that I can recommend to my clients such as

- Nutritionist
- Chiropodist
- Herbalist
- Jewellery maker (Probably less obviously synergistic, so let me explain. We swap news about where the next indulgence evenings are and have stalls next to each other so that we can

rave about each other to potential clients. People who like her jewellery tend to like being pampered!)

More recently, I met an image consultant called Elaine Boddy, who decided to set up a website (www.loveyourbody.me) to bring together a group of experts with a view to helping people to focus on loving their body, rather than beating themselves up for not being perfect. Through teaming up with synergistic businesses with this aim in mind, she not only has helped a lot of people to love their body, she's also pooled resources with those experts and has been able to realise an even bigger vision than if she'd tried to do all this on her own.

As well as benefiting from being able to run much larger events, the team are able to benefit from a stronger buying position through negotiating group discounts.

Action:

☑ Get to know synergistic service suppliers in your area and assess their reliability, honesty, integrity, and expertise. Remember that in recommending them, your reputation is also at stake so you need to make sure that you are happy recommending them.

☑ Before buying, see if you can enjoy greater discounts by teaming up with others and buying in bulk

Networking

I did mention networking briefly in the section about preparation where I recommended you set up your support network.

However, it's worth reiterating here, because it's such an important marketing tool and often overlooked by the small business as being a waste of time. I absolutely disagree on many levels.

Networking can be used as

■ a source for new clients
■ a source for finding services that you need to help your business
■ a forum for bouncing ideas amongst like-minded people and benefiting from their business experiences
■ a bit of fun to help you build up your social life!

I'm a natural networker. I love meeting people and I talk to everyone. Even people in the check-out queue. So networking comes easily to me.

If you're not naturally great at networking, you could consider joining a formalised network group who will have a set format so that you can learn what is expected and watch others so you can learn how to do it better. The more you do it, the more comfortable you get doing it and the easier it becomes so it's a good place to start.

There are plenty to choose from. Usually you pay a joining fee, an annual fee and pay for your meal at each event. They're a source of contacts to help you with your business needs, to help refer clients to you and you to them, and a way of feeling a part of a wider community.

Some networks you could consider (and there are others) are:
www.theathenanetwork.com
www.wibn.co.uk
www.bni-europe.com

You don't have to join straight away – usually they allow you to go as a visitor to one or two meetings before you have to decide. That way you can get a feel for how they operate and whether it's for you. Give it time. The first time I went to one after I'd gone solo, I felt really uncomfortable because the formal networks appeared to be so *businessy* and I thought that I had escaped from that environment. I nearly didn't go back. Yet, the second time I went, I was much more comfortable, and this time I decided I would connect on a personal rather than a business level. Consequently, I came away with a few new clients and had helped to connect some of my own contacts with some of the people there.

If standing up in front of a crowd at a formal network event isn't for you, there are breakaway groups where you can meet for a coffee and a chat. I even know of one enterprising soul in my area who got fed up with having to pay to meet the people she wanted to network with, so set up her own get-together to meet every third Wednesday at a coffee shop in a book store and jokingly dubbed it "Women Wot Latte"! There's no joining fee, it's informal, and there's a constantly shifting group of people who attend as the word spreads.

When you are networking at a formal gathering you will need
- Name Badge – mine says "footreading.com, Jane Sheehan" because I want them to know what I do before they know my name. What I do is easier to remember and spell than my name is and therefore when they get back to their office they can look it up on the internet.
- A stack of either business cards or leaflets. You'll need to make sure everyone you meet gets one and if they have a friend or

colleague who might be interested, you may want to give them some spares. In the early days I went to network events just to socialise and I often forgot to take my leaflets with me, so now I keep a stash in my car so I've always got some with me!

■ Work out a very short but catchy description of what you do to capture people's interest.

A great example of a network event pitch:
A lady stood up and showed us a magic box. It looked just like a jewellery box.   She showed us a piece of paper on which there were lots of different numbers. She said "I take this piece of paper with lots of meaningless numbers on it. I put it in my magic box" (She put it in her box). "I pour on the fairy dust" (as she shakes glitter over the paper) "I shut the lid, and knock three times on it with my magic wand as I say the magic words" (she opens the box) "then as if by magic, I produce a full set of accounts and help you understand all those previously meaningless numbers". (With a flourish she produces a neat set of accounts from the magic box.) "My name is Kassia Gardner, contact me for all your book-keeping needs at www.bright-angels.co.uk".

■ Clarity on why you are attending. At some network events that I attend, I go with the purpose of meeting someone who can provide a specific service. I ask for recommendations. (That's how I found the graphic designer for my last book.) Sometimes I go with the purpose of finding new business. I ask for the specific type of client I am looking for. Last time, I asked for case-studies and stories about business issues, both bad and good experiences to help me write this book! Identify your key message and make sure you ask for what you want. I've seen a person turn up and say "I want the contact name of the buyer of meat at Tescos". You can be **that** specific. There's always someone who knows someone….

One of my friends, Vanessa Edwards, is circulating her prayer for world peace. She asked us all if we could help her spread them around the world. In just asking she's distributed 30,000 cards and knows that they have reached an impressive list of politicians, peace activists and celebrities. Don't underestimate the power of asking the people you know to help spread the word. (Request your copy of her Prayer for World Peace from www.vandaehworks.co.uk)

The last time I went to a formal networking event, I picked up three new pieces of business, and gained stories for this book. There is a section at the end of the network event where people say with whom they want to do business or give a mini testimonial about someone there. I had so many testimonials that it really boosted my self-confidence. Sometimes you forget that what you do is appreciated and it's so lovely to get the feedback. So another bonus of a formal networking event is that, if you are feeling at a bit of a low ebb (and who doesn't get like that from time to time), the testimonial part of the event can do you the world of good!

Of course there are also free internet-based resources that allow you to network such as
www.facebook.com
www.WeCanDo.biz
where you can network without leaving your desk. For me though, it doesn't really beat the face-to-face scenario.

Don't forget that you can use your own website to network. I have a forum where people are able to discuss foot-related issues. It's a way of sharing knowledge and keeping in contact with interested parties. Blogs are another way.

Kit of Butterfingers was nervous about her first time at The Athena Network. A friend suggested that she just bring along small samples of her cake and let the product speak for itself. She stood up and told us that when she was young she had a mother who grew her own vegetables, served organic food and cooked wholemeal pastry. Kit wanted the frivolity and fun of baking, keeping the same ethos of the best ingredients. The words she gave us were interesting enough, but when she produced cake boxes and our eyes fell on the sumptuously presented cupcakes inside, chocolate cakes with cream and strawberries on top, lavender cakes with purple icing and a sprig of lavender on top, carrot cakes, row upon row of beautifully presented, melt-in-the-mouth delicacies. We were sold. Sometimes letting your potential clients have a sample experience of what you are offering will go a long way to persuading them to become customers. I have no idea what the cost was of supplying a cake per person, but I know that I placed a £19 order with her the next day!

You reap what you sow

Apart from networking, it's always worth remembering that you reap what you sow. Do one thing each day that relates to spreading the word about either your business, or your knowledge. When I notice someone in pain, I often ask about the problem and then show that person how to work the reflexes themselves to help relieve the pain. I don't do it to get new business; I do it because I genuinely don't like to see people suffering and if possible, I'd rather see them help themselves than suffer in silence. However, I have noticed that you often get referrals as a result of random acts of kindness. It certainly helps to demystify what you do.

Opportunities under your nose?

Welcome pack

When you first get a client, it's useful to offer them a welcome pack. In it you can provide

- information about your various services
- details of your cancellation policy
- details of your business guarantees
- details of any special offers
- details of any products available for purchase
- testimonials from satisfied customers

Consider offering your new clients an incentive to promote your services. "Word of mouth" is the cheapest and most effective form of advertising. Wouldn't it be great to formalise the process and deliberately make it work for you? One friend of mine offers a "Recommend a Friend" voucher where they write their own name and address on one side of the voucher, then hand the voucher to a friend. The voucher offers the friend a discount off their first treatment on production of the voucher. When my friend has received payment for the treatment, and a copy of the voucher, he is then able to contact the person on the back of the voucher to offer them a discounted treatment as a thank you for their recommendation.

Other ideas are "Buy one, get one half price" which you could introduce with a validity for periods when you are traditionally quieter.

For all these offers, it is worth making the offer tangible in the form of a letter, an invitation or a voucher.

Write down a list of the people who are already advocates of your services. Who praises you to the hilt? Who value what you do? On reviewing the list, work out a way of incentivising them so that they benefit each time someone acts on their recommendation. If they are singing your praises without any incentive, imagine how much more they might do with an incentive!

It's also worth asking what incentive they might like.

> ## Action:
> ☑ Create a welcome pack for new customers.
> ☑ Devise an incentive scheme.

Infect others with your enthusiasm

There is nothing more attractive than someone who is passionate and enthusiastic about something. They start to talk about their passion and you see them light up, become animated and you can't help but be drawn by their enthusiasm. Remember this next time someone asks you what you do and you feel those initial pangs of modesty or embarrassment about telling them. A half apologetic mutter about what you do just simply isn't going to work.

"Our deepest fear is not that we are inadequate. Our deepest fear is that we are powerful beyond measure. It is our light, not our darkness that most frightens us. We ask ourselves, Who am I to be brilliant, gorgeous, talented, fabulous? Actually, who are you not to be? You are a child of God. Your playing small does not serve the world. There is nothing enlightened about shrinking so that other people won't feel insecure around you. We are all meant to shine, as children do. We were born to make manifest the glory of God that is within us. It's not just in some of us; it's in everyone. And as we let our own light shine, we unconsciously give other people permission to do the same. As we are liberated from our own fear, our presence automatically liberates others."

– from ***A Return to Love***, by Marianne Williamson (www.marianne.com)

When you read the inspiring words above by Marianne Williamson, it makes you realise that you are not serving anyone by down-playing your talent.

Word of mouth

Earlier I told you about a "recommend a friend" scheme to be included in a welcome pack. The more you can get others to talk about you and your services in a positive light, the better. You know that if someone tells you about this fabulous little café nearby, you pop along and try it next time you're there. You trust a friend's recommendation. If your services become a recommendation from a friend it's more likely to break down someone's resistance to trying something new.

What ways can you think of to generate that recommendation?

I've often attended seminars where at the beginning of the seminar they ask you "what one thing do you think you will get out of this seminar?" And as they teach you a few things they then say "Write down 3 things in your own words that you have learned today that you can put into practice".

By doing this, they've set your expectation that you will get something out of the seminar and made sure that you will listen more effectively when they get to the relevant point for you. They have made you concentrate on recognising what it is you have learned. When you get home and review your notes, you'll pay the most attention to that list of three things.

Well, why not introduce a similar idea in your business. Ask the client what they expect, before they try your service. Then after they have tried the service, ask them to evaluate the experience.

In asking what they want, you may learn of gaps in your service that you can add to the package you offer.

Action:
- ☑ Explore ways of generating recommendations for your service.
- ☑ Ask the client what they expect from your service then surpass those expectations.

Community events

What's going on in your community? The more you can tap into an existing community the easier it is for news about your service to spread. Check out your local papers and notice boards to see what's happening in your area. Are any of the events suitable for you to use to present your services, offer samples or taster treatments of your work, or just for you to leave a few flyers at?

Looking in my local paper this week here are some of the events:

- Race for Life
- School Dance
- Village Fete
- Women's Institute meeting
- Music Festival

Although the Race for Life event is a sponsored run to promote a cancer charity, there is a chance for you to promote your services there if you do sports massage or reflexology. Pre-race you could promote your services as a way of getting in optimum shape or for honing mental attitude for the race. During the race you can offer taster treatments to the spectators and after the race you can offer a specialist service for the runners.

Does the school dance have a printed programme? Could you advertise your services in it? Could you go along to network with attendees? Schools offer a close community of Mums who talk to each other – a great opportunity to get the "word of mouth" marketing going.

Village Fetes are a great opportunity for you to set up a stall and offer taster treatments. Be aware of having to adapt to the outdoor conditions. Take heavy stones to act as paperweights so your flyers don't blow away. Maybe have a tent or a gazebo in case of inclement weather. Change the way you put up display boards so that you can tie them down so you don't spend the rest of the day chasing them round a field with every sudden gust of wind (you can tell I speak from experience here!)

Women's Institute meetings offer an opportunity for you to present yourself as a speaker. They have an annual programme of speakers who give interesting talks on a variety of subjects. Give the talk, but also have a call to action such as a "book today and get xyz free". Also take your "recommend a friend" vouchers.

Sometimes you'll attend a local event in the hope that you'll generate business, but when you get there, you may find that for one reason or another, you get no customers. It happens. Do NOT, repeat NOT get despondent. This is not the disaster you anticipate. There is always an opportunity and you are always sowing seeds for your future. It just means that there are no takers at that moment. You still have a job to do to get your face known, build awareness of your service's existence and to put out a professional and positive image despite the lack of immediate sales.

I was invited at the last minute to share a corner of a friend's stand at a village music festival. The idea was we'd offer taster treatments during the day, but we would shut up shop for the evening to be able to enjoy the entertainment for free afterwards. The weather was terrible and despite our best efforts I didn't have any paying customers at all that day. This is highly unusual for me. But I made sure that I spoke to everyone who passed my stall, explained what I did, handed them a leaflet, and luckily my friend also chipped in with "she's amazing" and other such testimonials. It can be hard to keep your spirits high when there are no customers. We told jokes to each other, swapped treatments on each other, and generally made sure we were having a great time. Don't allow yourself to fall into the trap of a negative spiral. There's always a learning curve, an opportunity and a great experience to be had, even if it's not the one you anticipated.

Half way through the day, the compere came round announcing all the concession stalls on the public address system. "We've got a tombola, a jewellery stall, a foot reader.....Foot reading? What's that?" So I took the microphone from him, and proceeded to explain whilst using his feet as an example. Luckily he was wearing open sandals. As I handed the microphone back, I told him some more personal things that he wouldn't want amplified round the field.

Later that evening, after we'd shut down our stalls and were enjoying the entertainment, the compere came over to see me. He explained that he managed a business with 300 employees and had immediately telephoned his Human Resources Manager after his foot reading, to tell him what I'd revealed just by looking. He asked me about my pricing structure and how it would work for a corporate event. So was it worth my spending all day in a cold, damp field with no customers? You bet! Plus, because my friend and I were determined to have fun, we'd thoroughly enjoyed ourselves despite everything.

Learn the lesson. Just because the event isn't going the way you'd envisaged, don't give up hope. You are always sowing seeds and you can't always anticipate how they will grow.

When you decide to attend a local event, don't rely on the organisers to do all the advertising. Sure, they will advertise the event. But you need to do your own marketing beforehand. Tell all your existing customers. Put posters up advertising that you will be there and what you are going to be doing. Mention it in your newsletter. Tell everyone you know. You need to create a buzz about you and about your stand so that when you arrive you're not sitting around doing nothing. It's another excuse to get your name in front of your potential and existing customers, a reason to communicate with them. Don't forget to take your diary to offer appointments after they've had a taster treatment.

> ## Action:
> ☑ Check your local papers to look for business opportunities.
> ☑ Consider how you can make the most of an event even when sales are poor

Cross-selling

It is more expensive to attract a new customer, than it is to service your existing customers well. Think carefully about what you are offering in terms of service and products. Are your existing clients aware of all the services and products that you offer?

There may be an opportunity for you to cross-sell products and services to your existing clients. This will help increase your turnover and hopefully your profits. Don't get complacent. Just because you know all the services and products you offer doesn't mean that your client does. Your customer will see this as a positive service to themselves if it is presented properly.

> ## Action:
> ☑ Ensure all clients are aware of all your services and products.
> ☑ Consider how you can tempt them to try one of your other services/products.

How to sell without selling

I'm not so keen on having someone sell me something in an obvious manner. Consequently, I don't like doing the direct sell approach myself. I'd rather just chat to someone and learn about them. If appropriate I'll mention how I wrote a book, or how I can read personality and emotion through the feet. But I won't blunder straight in and try a direct sell. Maybe this is a good sales technique – doesn't everyone like to think that the decision to buy is their own?

> When I give a free talk, I'd like to sell some of my books to help cover the cost of travelling to the event. To enable this to happen, I use a 6ft trestle table on which I place my laptop and projector. Next to my equipment I also place my books with a small sign saying what they are and how much they are.
>
> As I give the talk, I have the books constantly in front of the audience so that they can have the length of the talk to decide whether they want to buy a book or not. I've made them aware that the books exist. I've made them aware of the price and through giving a taster of what I'm about through the talk, I've made them aware of whether they want to know more or not.

Some ways of selling without selling:
- Offer a taster of what you do or a demonstration.
- Generate word of mouth interest.
- Set up a tempting display.

To advertise or not to advertise?

Before you can decide whether to advertise, you need to know what your marketing and advertising budget is. Without knowing how much you can spend, you'll make terrible choices. When you first start your business, you'll be making guesses about how much income you will have and then dividing that figure into budgets for all your other expenses. After you've started your business, you'll be better able to understand the incoming and outgoing expenditure. At this point you will need to calculate the amount you spend on advertising and marketing, versus the number of new customers that you gain through that spend. Then you will know the maximum amount you can spend in order to attract new business. Most businesses try to get away with spending the least amount, but this is a false economy. Gaining customers is key to establishing a profitable business so you will need to ensure you market and advertise effectively.

- Take time to develop a strong offer with a clear and direct call to action.
- Invest time and effort in writing a good letter or advert and headline.
- Mention the benefits of your service. (Answer the reader's unspoken question of "What's in it for me?")

Marketing and advertising is a process, not an event. It's hardest to keep your marketing and advertising going when you are busy. So build a 12 month marketing calendar. Put on the calendar what you will do to attract new prospects. Put on your calendar what you will do for existing customers. For example, are there other products or services that you offer that the customer has not yet tried? It's important to keep a regular dialogue with your existing customers so that you can gain valuable feedback about your business. Where are the customers happy and where do they feel you need to try harder? It doesn't matter what you think, it's more important what they think because without them you wouldn't have a business.

Once you've placed an advert in the media, you will receive phone calls in the future from those publications. The answer to whether you are willing to place an ad with them is always "No" unless you've pre-planned it in your marketing plan and therefore in your marketing budget. If you have already planned it in your marketing plan, then their phone call presents you with an opportunity to negotiate to get the best discount.

Should you even be advertising? As soon as I say advertising, you're probably thinking of placing an advert in a publication. That's one of the more expensive ways of advertising. When you first start your business you'll probably not have such a big budget and will need to get a lot more creative about how you advertise. It's really easy to design and print a leaflet about your services. You could begin by giving such a leaflet to all your existing contacts – family, friends, and friends of friends. If you offer a call to action such as a discount for a limited period only, a two for one offer, or similar, then you can stimulate new business for very little outlay. You could email your offer to your email contacts. In this way it would be easy for your email contacts to forward the offer to more people. Ask them if they would forward the offer. If you don't ask, you don't get. Does anyone in your support group have a newsletter in which you could place a small article about your services?

When you do decide to advertise and you have calculated your budget – consider which publications have a readership that matches your preferred customer. We've been experimenting with advertising in local village pamphlets with good success. Is there a local fete where you can place an advert in the programme? Is there a speciality magazine that relates to your customers' interests? Contact those publications and ask for

- Circulation figures (that's how many people will buy the publication)
- Readership figures (That's how many people will see the publication which may be a higher figure than circulation figures due to people sharing their copies etc)
- Date of publication
- Frequency of publication
- Deadline by which you need to have sent your advert
- Cost of placing advert and whether that includes free graphic design
- Is there a discount for placing the advert regularly?
- Is there a discount for running a test advert because you've never used that publication before?

I'm often asked if I think Yellow Pages, or Thompson's Local Directory or similar directories are worth considering. I'd ask you to consider how much it costs, then compare that cost with other forms of advertising. If you were to consider looking for someone with your own service offering, where would you search for that service? If the Directory is the first place you think of, then it would be worth considering. If the internet is the first place you think of, then maybe that should be your first consideration. In addition, consider whether you are in the main catchment area for that directory. I live in a very small village which is on the edge of the catchment area for the directory and I only received three enquiries in a year from advertising in the directory. Because I kept careful records about where my new customers were coming from, I was able to test the effectiveness of my advertising spend and change accordingly.

Action:
- ☑ Evaluate which media has readership to match your purposes
- ☑ Calculate your advertising budget
- ☑ Set up a marketing calendar for the year
- ☑ Write an effective advertisement
- ☑ Calculate the ratio between advertising spend and influx of new clients
- ☑ Test the success of different advertising by keeping records

Radio advertising

Radio allows you to focus your advertising on specific groups of people (by choosing a programme aimed at that age group or geographical location). It often costs less than other broadcast media. Most people listen to the radio. On average, people say they listen to the radio for at least two hours per day every day.

If there is more than one radio station in your area, they will specialise in entertaining specific age groups, lifestyles, and subject interests. Because of this, you can ensure your advertising spend is focused tightly on the group you want to reach.

It's important to target a station that reaches your best group of customers. A top 40 or pop station will appeal to teenagers and 18 to 24 year old women. Country stations pull in 25 to 54 year old men. A classic rock station would pull in 25 to 54 year old men. A news/talk station would specialise in an affluent audience over 55 years of age.

Check out the ratings information for any station or programme that you are considering. Consider carefully what the ratings info is saying. Radio advertising sales people have a job to put their radio station in the best possible light. Question the figures carefully. The old joke among radio programmers is "even though we don't have good ratings, we're number one with men aged 18-24 who have hair loss!"

Expect to pay more for peak listening times such as drive times. Expect to pay less overall if you purchase an advertising package combining different times of day or different days of the week. Some radio companies own several stations nationally. If this is the case, you could negotiate a package across the network of stations.

Some radio stations will produce your advert for you at no extra cost. In most cases, the person who sold you the advertising spot will also write your ad copy. It will be recorded by one of the station's DJ's.

Repeat your key message at least three times during the advert. End with your phone number or website or address – whichever is the easiest for the listener to remember. Often a phone number is written into a jingle so that the number becomes easier to remember as a song.

Ask to meet whoever is going to be recording your advert and bring along a free sample or gift for them. They are very busy people and you want them to be completely on your side. You don't want them to see your advert as just another one that they've got to get through.

When you buy an advertising package, see if you can get them to agree to have the DJ do the key messages live on air at least once. When they ad-lib live, they tend not to keep their eye as strongly on the clock as they would if it were pre-recorded so you may get them talking about it for much longer than you've paid. When I was first on radio, the café which I frequented had a live broadcast from their premises. I learned that if you have a suitable premises with a live audience (such as a store, salon with café or are based in a shopping centre) then you can often persuade the local radio station to send their roving reporter along. You may even be able to tempt them to do a two hour show from your location if you sell it right. Stations often bring with them attention-getters such as brightly painted vans, inflatable mascots or flags. Make sure you have plenty of staff on hand to help convert visitors into buyers.

My PR lady, Alison McCalpin, organised a joint swimming, cycling and running club event in Ely. The purpose (and outcome) was to create a renewed interest in those three clubs from local people and to increase numbers wanting to join. They staged a triathalon relay, obtained sponsorship from Specsavers, and invited the local radio station along to cover the event. (They also invited celebrity foot reader, Jane Sheehan, to read the feet of the runners, but that's another story!) The outside broadcast vehicle arrived emblazoned with the radio station's logo. They set up two flags that could be seen from a distance. Even better, they'd been plugging that they were going to be there for weeks beforehand. The event was a success in that they gained public interest in the three clubs and saw a swell in the membership numbers.

Test your marketing and advertising

The secret of great marketing is testing. Start with a small sample, measure how it is working, then when you've tweaked it to be as effective as you can, scale up the marketing. Measure your results. In this way, you can better calculate in the future what is the most that you need to spend to get a new client.

Having a tear off coupon and marking that coupon with a different code per media placement means you can test where the lead came from.

When I worked in direct marketing, we worked to a 1 to 2% conversion rate. By that I mean if we sent out 100 pieces of mail we'd expect 1 or 2 people to respond. This is the figure you can expect if you're contacting a general list or database. That conversion rate can become much higher if they are existing customers or qualified leads. Thus you can see why the marketing professionals tell you it is expensive to attract new customers, and recommend that you do everything in your power to service the customers you already have.

Action:
- ☑ Plan your marketing/advertising schedule.
- ☑ Consider how you can test your advertising.

Conversion rates

Know your conversion rate and how to improve it. By that I mean how many people show an interest in your services and how many of those interested parties then go on to make a booking with you?

To improve your conversion rate, always ask for the appointment/ order more than once. It usually takes people to see something seven times before they even register that they've seen it.

Follow up. Persistence pays off. How many times have you been to a pamper evening when you really enjoyed the treatment, get home meaning to contact the therapist to book a treatment, then life gets in the way. If they were to follow up on having met you, they may be able to convert your interest more easily into a booking.

Create a sense of urgency in your potential customer to buy now. What will they miss out on if they don't buy now? Every time I make an overseas tour, in the run up to that tour I get much busier because my regulars know that I won't be around for a while and they try to squeeze in an extra treatment before I leave. Put time limits on any special offers that you give. It's easy to go from full price to zero but not so easy from zero to full price!

Make sure your prospective customers know your unique selling point. Why should they buy from you rather than your competition?

When talking to prospective clients, ask better questions. It helps to build a rapport with them, and above all, listen to their answers. Learn how to build a better rapport with your potential customers. Understand their buying style.

Understanding potential customers' buying styles

Buyers have many different likes, dislikes and motivations. You need to determine the likes, dislikes and buying styles of your potential customers and to adapt your communication style to match them.

Some buyers
- Like to have fun.
- Like new products.
- Like proven products.
- Like a lot of data.
- Like you to be direct.
- Like personal talk.
- Like time to think.
- Like to negotiate.
- Like showy products.
- Like traditional products and
- Some don't…

There are four distinct behavioural styles.

The Driver

This is a very bottom line, cut to the chase, type of customer. They are direct, forceful, aggressive, decisive, competitive, results oriented, impatient and are quick decision makers.

They are primarily interested in the answer to the question **"What can you or your product or service do for me?"**

When communicating with these customers, be clear, specific and to the point. Don't ramble or waste their time. They are interested in new and innovative products and services. Stick to business and avoid any effort to socialise or chit chat.

The Social

They are very talkative, socially engaging, enthusiastic, charming, gregarious, optimistic, inspiring, and tend to be impulsive decision makers.

They are primarily interested in the answer to the question **"Why should I do business with you or your company instead of someone else?"**

When communicating with these folks allow time for some socialising and don't be cold or curt. Ask them questions that allow them to talk about their goals. Don't dwell on facts and figures. Provide testimonials from people they view as important or prominent.

They are interested in new, showy, and innovative products and services.

The Amiable

They are relaxed, serene, non-demonstrative and are shy and hesitant to open up or share any information about themselves or their situation.

Because they are hesitant and slow to develop trust they want to know **"Who else in my field are you working with?"**

When communicating with these buying styles patiently listen and be responsive. Provide plenty of proof and statistics. Take it slowly and easily and don't force a quick decision.

They are slow decision makers who like traditional, proven products, guarantees and assurances.

The Analytical

This person is methodical, very sceptical, cautious, evasive, analytical, systematic and precise. They will ask a lot of questions and not want to reveal much of anything.

They are perfectionists who want to know **"How does this exactly work?"** and **"Why is it done that way?"** and **"What data do you have to support your claims"?**

Because of their exacting nature they tend to be in such professions as accounting, architecture, banking, engineering and law.

When communicating with these potential customers approach them in a direct, straightforward way and be very specific. Have data to support everything you say. Use a logical approach. Present specifics and details. Provide them with the information and the time they need to make a decision.

They need a lot of proof and background information and they need plenty of time to absorb and digest facts before making a purchasing decision.

They are extremely slow decision makers and are highly suspicious of new and unproven products. When presenting to them use plenty of research information and testimonials.

Questions for you to consider
- What is your natural selling style?
- Which buying style is the most difficult for you to connect with?
- Which style do you tend to avoid?
- What do you need to do to become a more skilled communicator?

How quickly can you respond to a potential customer's query? My assistant Sarah systemised a lot of my sales processes so that I could improve my response time to enquiries about my foot reading workshops. She noticed that I was regularly typing the course content, and details about how to book, from scratch. In having pre-prepared templates it helped speed up the whole process; it cut down the time I spent too and as we all know, time is money!

Beware of over-systemising. I've had dealings with companies where every contact with them results in a template email being sent to me. When trying to resolve a problem, this approach can be downright irritating. Imagine receiving yet another response to a heartfelt plea for a resolution that begins "Dear Vendor...." There's a fine line between systemising for efficiency and leaving your customers feeling as if you don't care about them individually or you haven't read their original query.

Action:
- ☑ Understand buying and selling styles and motivations.
- ☑ Write adverts accordingly.
- ☑ Systemise your processes whilst maintaining the personal touch.

Direct response

When you first start out, you may prefer a direct response mechanism. By this I mean, you make an offer to potential clients asking them to quote a reference or present a voucher and then note the success of the response to the offer.

By using a direct response mechanism means that you can get the marketing to pay for itself. You need to know who your target market is and how to reach them. In other words, who is your ideal customer and what offer would tempt them to try your services. It's also easy to test response to offers by placing the same offer in different media.

Include a call to action, and have the response coded so that you can see what piece of marketing prompted the customer to act.

For example, my brother owned a fish and chip shop and the fun fair opposite closed down. He had to find new customers. He had a series of leaflets made, each one offering a different voucher, some saying produce this voucher and get a free cup of tea or coffee, some offering a percentage saving and some saying "buy one get one half price". As the new customers started turning up at his shop with the vouchers he was able to see which offer got the best response and use the information for any future marketing that he undertakes. Incidentally, he has noticed that the demographic profile of his customers has changed as a result of his marketing efforts. The unit spend per customer had increased. This was an unexpected side effect but very useful to know.

What he also found was that not everyone redeemed the voucher so for those cases he'd not only gained new customers but received the full price too.

> ## Action:
> ☑ Write a direct response advert or letter or leaflet.
> ☑ Include a response code.
> ☑ Experiment with different offers to gauge the response.

Other forms of advertising

Apart from advertising in newspapers, magazines and on the radio, perhaps you could consider less obvious forms of advertising:

Car

Why not have your car act as a form of advertisement for you? I travel the length and breadth of the country and have had my car turned into a mobile advertising platform! I can be travelling on the motorway, minding my own business, when a vehicle will pass and the passengers will put their feet up at the windows! So has my advertising worked? Did they notice it? Will they be talking about it? You bet!

For my birthday, my parents bought me some personalised car number plates. All of a sudden, more people were noticing my car advertising. How they missed the large foot and the white writing before, I'll never know, but it certainly seems that the number plates have increased the advertising recognition. (My number plate is J55 TOE). I'm not, however, tempted to have a fibreglass foot on my roof! You can take things too far!

At a recent workshop, someone asked me how effective was it as a form of advertising, then spent the rest of the day watching people walk past and stopping to read it!

When I do it again on my next car, I will put the website name first and make it bigger and remove the letters after my name. I'm fed up with having to explain what they mean!

You may be wondering whether it is embarrassing to have your info all over your car. Well, you get so used to it, and even forget it's there. I often turn up at pamper evenings and have the organiser run over and greet me by name and I'm very impressed that they recognise me, forgetting that it would be very easy to do so just by reading the car!

When I've been on a long trip, I like to check my book orders on my return to see whether new book orders have arrived from the areas I've just visited. It's a good way to see how effective my advertising was.

And yes, there have been occasions when I've had the odd dodgy phone call, but they are few and far between.

Remember, if you do decide to place advertising on your car you must keep your car clean both inside and out as it is now an ambassador for your company. Plus, if you have vinyl lettering you have to hand-wash the car as machines would easily remove it.

Don't place any unnecessary stickers (especially humorous ones) on the vehicle. I remember parking next to an electrician's van where he had a sticker saying "Hard work never hurt anyone, but why take the chance." I often wonder if he has lost business through it.

Do park your car in a prominent position so that the advertising can be seen. An alternative would be to use removable magnetic signs.

Magnets

One of my colleagues, Phil Nuttridge, has had some fridge magnets produced on which there are body-work exercises and his contact details. As a massage therapist, he can give the client the fridge magnet as a visual prompt for the exercise he wants to set them as homework. Then, by placing the magnet on their fridge, they now have a constant, visual, reminder of him and his work. The perceived value may be higher to the client than the actual cost of producing them.

Sign writing

No-one can come to you if they don't know you are there. Look at the outside of the building where you work. Is there an opportunity to put up a sign, or poster or banner to indicate you are there? Can you place a sandwich board outside? Can you put a sign in the garden? Are you missing an opportunity to let people know you exist?

You may need planning permission to put up a permanent sign. You can find out about this by contacting your local council. Ask them what their definition of "permanent" and "temporary" is.

T-Shirts

T-shirts and clothing are another form of advertising. When I worked in Hawaii, I missed using my car as a mobile advertising board. I was wandering around the island anonymously, trying to drum up interest in my workshops. So I had some t-shirts made saying "Footreading. com" on the front and emblazoned on the back was "stop me for a foot reading!"

I have a friend who always wears a white uniform for treatments. He had some made with his business name embroidered on the front, just below where he pins his nurse's watch. Popping out to Tesco's one day, a person in the queue, noticing his business name, struck up a conversation about what he did and decided to book an appointment!

What you wear and how you wear it can make or break your business. Why not choose to wear it deliberately and be your best form of advertising. Keep your outfit clean, pressed and looking new. If it starts to look tired, replace it.

Public Relations (PR)

What is it and who is it for?

What is public relations and why should a holistic business be involved?

Most people think that public relations is just about writing and sending out a press release to the media. It's so much more than that.

Simply put, your business is all about people. Who are the people who come into your sphere of influence or who influence your business? Who are the people who may be affected directly or indirectly by your business? Those people may be

- your customers
- your neighbours who may be affected by your business (increased traffic, parking, noise)

- the wider community (people who like your kind of service and people who are outright hostile towards it)
- legal bodies, trade associations and other lobbyists

Public relations is simply managing the communication between your business and the people it comes into contact with.

In my business I have different mechanisms in place so that I can regularly communicate with each of these groups. For my customers, potential customers and students I have a monthly newsletter called

"The Pampering Times". In it I include articles of interest, news about my services and classes, and positively encourage my customers and students to contribute. You may want to find other ways to communicate regularly with your customers through

- open days
- letter or email about new offers or services
- reminder service (for example calling the customer the day before their appointment to remind them of the time)
- birthday card to regular customers

With the wider community I have joined network events, do pamper evenings where I can show what I do through taster treatments, and keep an eye on the press and trade publications to stay up-to-date about any issues that may arise, laws being introduced, taxation changes etc. I also have membership to a related therapy and trade association. I donate some of my time to a locally-based charity. In the early days of setting up, I also gave free talks about my business to local community groups. You may want to

- join a trade association
- join a network group
- give talks or write articles to local community groups/publications
- sponsor a local activity
- donate a percentage of your profits or a day of your time to a local community-based charity
- get involved in setting up indulgence evenings with local schools, giving taster treatments

In addition to all of the above, I also hire a public relations expert. I used to work for a public relations agency so you may wonder why I go to such expense when I already have the skills to do it for myself. The answer is simple – it's much easier for someone else to sell you than it is for you to sell yourself. I always felt it sounded like bragging and immodesty when I did it. The additional advantage of hiring a

PR expert is that we can keep the momentum going when I'm too busy to do it myself.

Recognise that your PR is part of your team. You work together with joint aims and focus on what you want to achieve. Agree a budget, visualise the outcome and be specific and realistic with your aims. If you can't picture yourself doing it, then don't waste your time or money.

As well as all the above, you can also write press releases!

Action:
☑ Consider which groups of people your business affects.
☑ Choose a mechanism for addressing each group.

How do you write a press release?

The media (by that I mean newspapers, magazines, TV, radio etc) look for anything that is

- new
- best
- innovative
- biggest
- first

When writing a press release, these are the aspects that you will highlight in order to interest the media into choosing to publish it. Where your "news" does not fit into these superlatives, you could issue results of a survey to highlight what you want to impart. Statistics can often get you published. So too can a fantastic photograph that is impactful and tells a story. On a slow news day, the photograph may get you the coverage that you seek even if the story is weak.

When writing the press release, remember that the journalists tend to cut the story from the bottom up, so ensure that your main news is at the beginning, and the "nice to have but not essential" news is further down the press release.

Include a quotation from a key spokesperson. Direct quotations can't be edited, only used in full or left out completely by the journalist, so make sure you quote some salient points that are key to the article!

Indicate the press release is finished by typing "ENDS" then follow up with some key background information about you and your business and the relevant contact details.

Example of a press release

Manor Beeches
Manor Gardens
Maids Moreton
Buckinghamshire
MK18 1QA

Draft press release #2
Date: 14.10.2005
For general release
Approved by:...

WHAT ARE OUR FEET TELLING US?
New book shows us how to 'read our feet'

Jane Sheehan, TV's celebrity Foot reader, has launched a new book to show us all the hidden messages in our feet. 'Let's Read Our Feet!' shows us how the shape of our feet and toes can not only tell us a lot about our personalities, but also help us to improve areas of our lives that we are unhappy with.

Reflexologists use foot reading to understand their clients from a more holistic perspective. It is used as a therapy to help people identify issues in their life and help them move forwards.

Jane launched her career this Easter, with an appearance on ITV's This Morning, where she read celebrities' feet and demonstrated how our feet give away our true selves.

Jane comments: "We are all used to changing our facial expressions and hiding our true feelings, but we can't do that with our feet – they tell the truth! Simply by analysing the shapes of feet and toes, we can tell an awful lot about a person. By using the guidelines set out in my book, you can amaze your family and friends by exposing their hidden selves. You can also take it further and use foot reading as a self-help guide to improving your control over your own life. It's a great tool for personal development."

Jane's new book illustrates how the toes and shape of the foot signify fears, feelings and personality traits. For example, if the second toe does not touch the floor, that person has lost his way in life and is not getting what he wants anymore, but may not be aware of what it is he actually DOES want. Puffiness at the base of the fourth toe indicates problems in relationships that they want to talk about but aren't doing. If the big toe bends towards the little toe, that person is doing too much for others and not enough for themselves. This can be tested by the changes in that toe when they start to find time for their own interests - the toe will start to move back.

Let's Read Our Feet! is designed to help reflexologists and other therapists with an interest in the area to develop new skills, but it has been written to appeal to anyone with no previous knowledge of reflexology or foot reading to enjoy.

The book is available through Jane's website www.footreading.
com or through Amazon and is priced at £14.99 plus p&p.
- ENDS -

About the author

Jane first became interested in foot reading after a reflexology
session had a profound impact on her, and she decided to find out
more about the link between feet and wellbeing. She developed
her foot reading skills through a combination of experience and
learning from specialist sources. After four years of practising
reflexology and foot reading in her spare time, Jane left her nine-
to-five office job in April 2005 and embarked on a career centred
on her foot reading skills.

Her abilities were immediately picked up by ITV's This Morning,
when they asked her to demonstrate her skills live on the
programme, reading celebrities' feet. Further TV and radio work
followed, and she recently appeared in Channel 4's Big Brother's
Little Brother, reading the housemates' feet.

She now holds regular seminars across the country, and hosts
Foot reading Parties (the modern alternative to commercial
'cosmetics sales' parties for today's busy lifestyles) as well as
continuing with her reflexology work.

For more information on Jane and her work, please go to www.
footreading.com
Or telephone Alison McCalpin PR 01353 659564

Writing the press release and sending it isn't enough. You will get the
best results if you telephone to sell-in the idea of publishing it. Also,
you'll very quickly realise if the story is of interest or a non-starter.

It is worth finding out the deadline dates for each publication. It would be best to avoid contacting any of the journalists on deadline day as their attention will be focused on finishing the publication rather than on you.

Some local newspapers (for a small donation to their favourite charity) will be willing to let you spend a day with them watching the process, from start to finish, of putting together the newspaper. This is a very worthwhile exercise as you will gain a much better insight into the whole process. When I visited, they even had a file of "bad" press releases which they showed us as an example of "what not to do!"

After receiving a press release a journalist may ring you to interview you. When you are going to be interviewed, it is best to rehearse your key messages. What are the main points that you want them to publish or broadcast? Once you're familiar with delivering this information in the most interesting way, you will then want to rehearse answering difficult and even hostile questions.

For example, I am regularly asked what I would say to anyone who thinks my therapy is a load of old hooey.

On radio shows I'm often faced with two presenters who do the old "good cop, bad cop" routine where one of them questions me from a positive angle and the other one interviews me from a very sceptical or sometimes hostile angle. The important thing to remember is that it is not personal, it is entertainment, so if you can inject humour into your answers, as well as being informative, honest and accurate, you will have no need to worry.

Occasionally the information you have presented will be edited to present the information in a different light than you originally intended. This is always the risk you run when you are not doing a live interview. That is why my preference is to do live broadcasts wherever possible. Should you be in the position where you have experienced such an editing, you will need to carefully consider damage limitation. Is it best to ignore the broadcast and chalk it up to experience or is it better to tackle the issue. This is where I find employing the experience of a public relations expert invaluable. They can guide you on the best course of action.

I pre-recorded a piece with MKTV where we went round a shopping centre reading the feet of the general public. Because it was going to be broadcast, I avoided saying anything too personal and kept the reading to general personality traits and things that would not embarrass them to have broadcast.

Some time later the item was broadcast and I was horrified to discover that they'd spliced my footage into a studio interview with a discussion about bad psychics. I am not psychic, never claim to be, and was horrified to be presented as if I was psychic. Also, I had not been given an opportunity to join in the discussion which would have allowed me to counter some of the comments.

How would you have handled such a situation? Would you have demanded a right to reply, posted a message about it on your own website or blog, or would you have ignored it?

Once you've sent out your press release, you never know where it may turn up.

I had a telephone call from my sister asking me if I knew I was in a book. "Yes!" I replied. "I'm mentioned in Donna Sozio's book *Never Trust a Man in Alligator Loafers* on page 150".

"No, not that one. One by Mark Frith, the ex-editor of Heat Magazine? Celeb Diaries?" she said.

Do you know that feeling when your stomach sinks? I couldn't think why I'd be in his book and I feared the worst! I rushed off to the nearest book store to find a copy and there on page 221, I found me. It was true. However, it wasn't as bad as I thought. It was mentioning a press release we sent him about reading feet at the Oscars.

Action:
- ☑ Write a press release.
- ☑ Consider your key messages.
- ☑ Consider how you will handle difficult or hostile questions.

Establish yourself as an expert

Your name is meaningless until your reputation is established. Until it is established, it's better to say your service first and then your name, so the reader knows "what's in it for me?"

If you can establish yourself as an expert in your field it will aid recognition of your name. If you have a very clear set of values and ethics that run through everything you do, then your reputation will be assured.

You may have seen therapists who are great proponents of the holistic health message, who speak to you at great length about good health habits and then you see them sneaking a cheeky cigarette behind their building. Or maybe you've met a consultant who tells you they believe in bringing honesty and integrity into the corporate workplace and then you are faced with them not paying their bills on time. Look carefully at your own business ethics and values and make sure that they are congruent with your actions. If you find a disparity between what you say you stand for, and what you actually do, this will damage your reputation and ultimately your profits.

I'm lucky, I have a good friend who tells me exactly what she thinks. She had a word with me about "now you're on TV, you've got to look the part all the time. You can't go out without any make-up on!" She's right. I am my business and I have to advertise it well in everything I say, do and even wear!

Action:
Consider how you can establish and maintain your reputation?

TV, radio and interview tips

I can remember the first time that I appeared on television. On the journey there I was petrified. A friend of mine telephoned me and asked me how I was and I admitted my fear. He asked me what I could see (a field through the train window, cows, trees) what I could hear (mobile phone going off in the carriage, sound of the train, people talking) what I could smell (coffee). In making me focus on the sensations in that moment, he helped me find a way to release the fear. Fear after all stands for false evidence appearing real! In focusing on the sensations, I was able to calm myself, focus on what was right in front of me and interrupt those whirling and unhelpful thoughts.

Since then, I use that technique before each show I do. It's still scary but it's much easier to cope with.

Ventriloquism on the radio?

My family laughed out loud the first time I told them that I was going to be doing foot reading on the radio. "Isn't that a bit like ventriloquism on the radio?"

It's probably one of the most effective things that I do to promote foot reading. When you watch television, you tend to select the programmes that interest you. When you buy a newspaper or magazine you tend to select the ones that more closely cover your interests. But when you listen to the radio you tend to have it on in the background and are more likely to stay tuned and listen in, even if it's not a subject you'd normally choose. So you're more likely to reach an audience who wouldn't otherwise select you.

When you listen to the radio, you feel as if the presenters are talking directly to you. It's a very intimate medium and as near to being able to emulate that therapist/client relationship on a large scale.

Sally Teixeiras, of Universallyrio.com, asked me to write an article about foot reading on the radio for her website at about the same time that I was preparing for a January radio show. I decided to use the example of preparing for that show to help me write the article. Here it is:

I was asked to appear on the Ted Robbins' radio show on BBC Radio Lancashire at 10.15am on 8th January 2009. I'd already been on the show once so we needed to find a new angle. Usually they are looking for interviews that are unusual, unique, topical or newsworthy. I'd already played the unusual and unique angle the first time I appeared on their show with very good results. Within minutes of explaining what foot reading is, and encouraging listeners to call in with their foot questions, the switchboard was fielding calls asking for foot readings live on air. This time, they were interested in the idea of "New Years Resolutions" – not surprisingly – it was January after all.

Before I even think what to say, I need to prepare my "key messages". I don't get paid to do radio interviews so I've got to make it work for me. I think about what messages I want the listener to remember and then prepare backwards from there. For example, do I want the listener to know the title of my book, the date of my next workshop or the name of my website?

My key messages:
- I will be available for foot readings in the Lancashire area from 9th to 12th January
- My website is www.footreading.com
- Details of my books and seminars are on www.footreading.com

It's best not to have too many key messages but rather to stick to just a few and repeat them often. I decide that if I only get chance to say one key message it will be my website address.

The radio station also has its key message. They will focus on "New Year's Resolutions".

So now I set about combining the two sets of messages to devise something that will work on the radio.

Key tips to remember for a radio interview are:

■ Make sure the microphone is near enough, especially if you are doing a live link from another studio. I was with a producer once when they didn't like the sound quality. They tried pressing lots of buttons to improve it, but in the end, they had to interrupt the interviewee to ask them to pull the microphone nearer. It made a vast improvement, but a lot of air time was lost through trying to rectify the problem. You don't want that to happen to you when it's such an easy thing to put right.

■ Imagine you are only speaking to one person. Avoid using phrases such as "all your listeners" or "any of you" and instead address the person directly. On Radio Two, Terry Wogan often reads out letters saying "your other listener mentioned…" implying that it's only Terry, the writer and one other person out there! Everyone knows that it's not the case, but it does add to the feeling of intimacy and the idea that the show is just for you.

■ The listener can not "see" what you are talking about, so describe it accurately so that they can imagine it. Appeal to all the other senses by conjuring sounds, smells, feelings, and visual images. Actually, when I think about it – if you're talking about feet, maybe mentioning smells is not such a good idea!

■ Rehearse the most common questions you think they will ask and practice adding your key message into the answers. For example:

> Interviewer: So Jane, what is foot reading?
>
> Me: In my book, "Let's Read Our Feet!" I explain how…..
>
> You get the idea. Its fun to listen to politicians being asked questions and how they side-step the question asked in order to deliver their key message.

■ Know who the audience is likely to be and tailor what you discuss accordingly. For example, if it is a breakfast show audience I won't be discussing fungal infections whilst they may be eating their cornflakes!

■ Sit up straight and smile – you can hear it in your voice.

- Aim to arrive early to the studio so that you can be cool, calm and collected. They know you are there and so you have the added advantage that they start plugging the slot. Once I got stuck in traffic on my way to the studio. I'd allowed an hour to cover a thirty minute journey but there had been a breakdown causing the traffic to be so bad that despite an early start, I was still ten minutes late. If you upset the interviewer they can set the whole tone of the interview. On the occasion I was late, they announced "it says here, Jane's most embarrassing moment was…"

- Wear your best outfit! Even though you are on the radio, you will feel more confident and it will come across in your voice. There have been a few occasions when, without warning, they have produced a camera and taken photographs for their website. Expect the unexpected and be prepared for anything!

- Send the producer of the show your biography, your press release and your key message and type in large print with one and a half line spacing. This is a tip I picked up from a radio station in Australia where the interviewer admitted that she actually needed glasses but was too vain to wear them. Because I'd prepared my information in large print she was able to use it despite the lack of "face furniture"!

- If it is a commercial radio station they will have less time for interviewing you as they will need to intersperse the interview with advertising and regular features. If it is a non-commercial radio station they may not allow you to mention your website as this may be seen as advertising. If this is the case, make sure they put details about you on their website so that people can find out more. One way I've found to overcome this is to say that I am "Jane Sheehan of footreading.com" as if that is my company name.

- Commercial radio stations often run competitions. (The BBC stopped after all the adverse press following a Blue Peter competition.) Sometimes you can donate a prize for a competition and it may gain you extra mentions on air. However, sometimes you may be charged an advertising fee for the privilege.

- Don't be fazed if they throw something unexpected at you. Just be honest. There's no shame in not knowing an answer.
- Don't upset the Producer of the show. I know of one company who can no longer appear on a certain station for trying to pull a fast one.

Give the listeners an added incentive to visit your website. I've placed a list of "the top 10 things that your feet say about you" on my website, so that I can direct listeners to find it.

Once I've decided upon my key messages, then I work out what kind of information I will be giving in the interview. There's often not much time to give huge amounts of information so I prepare small sound bites and pick a few ideas that I can bring into the conversation.

TV interview tips

TV interviews are similar to radio interviews in that you still need to prepare your key messages. Yet you've got the added problems of worrying about the visuals too.

When I've been on TV usually there is a researcher who contacts you prior to the show to give you a "mini audition" over the phone. Remember, they're looking for interesting TV so they won't want to be interviewing someone with no personality, one-word answers or a flat voice. The researcher will then pitch the idea to the rest of the team at their production meeting. If it gets the go-ahead then you may find yourself being invited onto the show.

- Be prepared – watch the show beforehand to get a feel for the format.
- Dress accordingly – having watched the show, what kind of clothing would be appropriate? When I was on Big Brother's Little Brother, two other interviewees had to have duct tape put over their clothing to hide fashion labels. So avoid wearing

anything that has a prominent logo. Avoid narrow stripes as they dance around on screen and are distracting. Notice the background colour on set and avoid wearing that colour.

■ Ensure your appearance is congruent. I remember watching a programme about reflexology where the therapist's nails were so long that I doubted they'd touched a client in a long time. If they had with nails like that, they'd have caused them a mischief!

■ Remember – everyone will judge you by your appearance. It's unavoidable. As soon as you appear on a TV set in someone's living room, they will feel it only fair to criticise you on your appearance. Even my best friends have felt the need to comment on "Why did you wear that?"

■ Audio – remember that they will want to put a microphone on you. Usually they clip a battery pack and transmitter/receiver to your waistband then feed the wire from the back, under your clothes, and clip the microphone to the front of your top. Be careful to place the microphone somewhere where your necklace won't keep hitting it. Knowing that you'll have to be "miked up" it would be more useful to wear a two piece outfit than a dress so that you have somewhere to clip the equipment.

■ Make-up – some shows have their own make-up artists. If this is the case, always take them up on their offer to do your make-up for you. This will ensure you look your best under the harsh lights. If there is no make-up artist, then wear a matt foundation – you don't want to look shiny under the lights. It's even more important to arrive early for a TV interview than for a radio interview so that you have time to ensure you have the best make-over.

■ Don't sit back in your chair – I noticed once when I was on "Inside San Diego" that the anchor woman never sat properly in her chair, but rather, perched on the edge. I realised that in this way you can keep the lines of your clothes looking good, and you look taller. If you sit back, you can look shorter, fatter and more crumpled.

■ Avoid wearing too bright a colour. High saturation colours, like red, can "bleed" on VHS videotapes.

Photograph tips

How many times have I seen a really good piece of publicity marred by an awful photograph? Don't underestimate the power of a really good photograph. It's definitely worth investing money into having a professional photograph of yourself taken for your sales literature and website. A photograph that is staged so that it also conveys visually a message about what you do is invaluable.

So how do you look fabulous on film?

■ Think "gorgeous" and you'll feel gorgeous. Apply your best make-up and use a matt finish so that you don't shine under the studio lights.

■ Imagine a hot guy (assuming you're a girl)! To avoid that rabbit-in-headlights expression, look at the camera as if it's the person you desire. If you think of someone you fancy it can give you a little twinkle in your eyes. If looking sexy is not the image you're after, then try thinking about the last time you succeeded at something and imagine the applause as you make your acceptance speech!

■ If blinking just as the picture is taken is a problem for you, then keep your eyes closed, count to three then open them in time for the photo. This works well if you are in the sun, as it helps you open your eyes for longer. I had to do a photo shoot whilst lying in flowers and I was suffering really badly from hay fever, plus the sun was right in my eyes. This is the technique I used.

■ Experiment with colour. Your portrait shots can look even more flattering in black and white or sepia and in the age of Photoshop you can have your photographs retouched so that you look as though you have the skin of an angel!

Action:
- ☑ Get a set of professional photographs to use for your advertising, PR and website.
- ☑ If you use them a lot, it's worth updating your photographs so that the readership is not tired of seeing the same pictures.

Telephone skills

Telephone skills

Answer machine versus answering service

When working in Hawaii, I asked my marketing agent what was the one tip that he thought every business should know. He said "Return all your calls". If someone leaves you a message and you don't respond, it can be a sure way of losing business. As technology gets more and more sophisticated, we can harness it to ensure our clients can always "reach" us. Even if we just have an answering machine.

What is the outgoing message on your answering machine? Does it match the needs of your business? At the very least it should announce what your business is, and when you will return their call.

As you are a holistic business, maybe it might be worth investing in an answering service so that there is always a human being at the end of the phone.

If you work from home, has every member of your household been trained on how to answer your business calls? If not, then maybe it should be house policy to let all calls go to answering machine so that you don't lose any calls or have any answered incorrectly. You may then return those calls as appropriate.

If someone is calling your business for the first time, what are the first impressions they will be left with?

Consider too, how many times does your telephone ring before the machine kicks in? Too soon and you may not reach it in time but too long and you may lose that all important call.

If working from home, you may want to obtain "Caller ID" on your landline. In this way, you can screen calls so that you only answer friends' and family on your time off and business calls during work time.

Turn off your phones' sound so that their ringing does not disturb clients.

Don't say "I'll ring you back ASAP" if you can't. Don't make promises you can't keep.

Telemarketing tips

Before I was a foot reader I had quite a variety of jobs. As a manager at a telemarketing agency, I learned things that would be very useful in most businesses.

Prepare

Before you pick up the phone to make a call, you need three pieces of preparation.

- **Work out who you need to speak to.** If you can find a name, even for a company you've never worked with before, it will help enormously. When you know the name of the person you are talking to, use it in the conversation. It puts the person at ease and makes you sound more professional.

- **Know the subject matter relating to the call.** Sounds like a no-brainer, but have you ever had a company ring you up where you've asked a basic question about the product they are trying to sell you, only to find that they know nothing about it and have to get someone else to ring you back. What kind of impression does that leave you with?

- **Prepare your lift pitch** – the idea of a lift pitch is that you are in a lift and have only the time between one floor and the next to sell your idea to the person in the lift with you. When on the phone, you may only have a few seconds to capture the listener's attention so you need to be able to grab their attention and hold it, whilst imparting the core message. When I worked in PR and rang journalists, we learned not to mention who we were or which PR agency we were from. We learned to grab their interest in our story first, then and only then would they be interested in our contact info.

■ **When ringing a new client back**, announce yourself as what you do first, then your name. "Hello, I'm the Reflexologist that you rang earlier – Jane Sheehan". Your name may not yet register with them.

Making the call

Some golden rules when making a call

■ **Smile while you dial.** Why? It lifts your voice, makes it sound more attractive to the listener. Make sure you're sitting up straight, and if you have "hands free", you may even want to stand up, if you need to put some authority into your voice. Where I worked, they even put up mirrors in front of you so you could see yourself during the call. Would you do business with someone who sounds depressed? Don't overdo it either. Would you do business with someone who sounds manically cheerful?

■ **Speak clearly.** Be careful to enunciate every consonant. Not all phone lines are clear and not all people you are ringing have good hearing. Every little helps.

■ **Actively listen.** Don't be thinking about what you want to say next. The information which that person is relating is important to them. If you're only listening for the bits that interest you, you'll be losing a lot of potentially useful information. Listen behind the words. What are they really telling you? It's useful to have a pen and paper by you to make notes, so that you can refer back to what they said, thus showing that they have been heard.

■ **Use open questions rather than closed questions.** Closed questions demand a yes or no answer. Open questions allow a wider answer. Listen very carefully to the answers. You can glean a lot of useful information that may not otherwise have been forthcoming. Open questions begin with

- ◆ Who
- ◆ What
- ◆ Where
- ◆ When
- ◆ Why
- ◆ How

Using open questions keeps it fresh, establishes the customer's needs, builds rapport, guides the conversation, shows you are listening and helps the person to feel heard. It encourages discussion. It presents a caring image which is exactly what you're trying to establish.

■ **Keep conversation relaxed and informative.** If you sense there is a tension that has crept into the conversation then there must be a reason. Be aware of the change. For example, have you had someone try to sell you a new mobile phone contract and you start off pleasantly but start to get irritated? If only the telemarketer picked up on that sooner, you wouldn't have slammed the phone down!

■ **Don't give up!** If you don't get through today, try tomorrow, or a month's time and keep trying.

Overcoming objections

It's not just what you say; it's how you say it. If you read a script, the person on the other end of the phone can tell. So don't! If you sound as if you've been ringing fifty other people that day and saying the same thing over and over again, you won't engage this person. Keep it fresh.

It's not just that you need to listen, it's how you listen. Subjective listening is when you listen just for the things that interest you. Active listening is when you listen to everything that's said and absorb it. When you are talking to someone, which form of listening would you prefer to hear and can you tell when they are doing one or the other? Yes, of course you can! I bet you can think of numerous examples where you lost patience with someone because you felt that they were only listening out for what they wanted to hear or jumping into the conversation too quickly before you'd fully had your say.

Telemarketers have a word for anyone who is paid to stop you getting through to the person to whom you want to speak. They call them "Gatekeepers". OK, maybe they call them some other choice words too, but we'll call them Gatekeepers here! If you've ever been in that role (and I have) then you will probably know most of the tricks that the telemarketers use to get past you. But sometimes you won't mind because they were so lovely. Another person may use the same trick on a different day and you won't let them through. The key for the telemarketer is to never give up and to stay polite and interesting. I asked Milton Keynes-based telemarketing expert, Jan Hardcastle (07876 508027) for her top tips on dealing with the "gatekeeper":

Key tips

- Pick up on the gatekeeper's accent and ask them about it.
- Use humour – it helps to build rapport.
- If the gatekeeper tells you they have a "no names policy" whereby they will not give out names, ask to be put through to the relevant department. Often staff elsewhere in the company aren't aware of the no-names policy, or even better, you get an answer machine where their name is freely given out! If you do get a live person, you can do your lift pitch and they may say "oh, that's not me you want, you want ...." If you're lucky enough for that to happen, ask for their direct line. Another idea is to ask for the email address of the relevant person in charge (email addresses are usually made up of someone's name!)
- If none of the above works, then ask which department to send a brochure, then ring back a few days later to check if they've received it. In that way, it's no longer a cold call, but is a little warmer.
- Have the courage to ask for what you want, be it an appointment, a name, an email address. If you don't ask, you don't get and what's the worst that can happen? They can only say no!

You are your reputation

Performance Ratin

Excellent

☒
☒
☒
☒
☒
☒
☒
☐

Good

☐
☐
☐
☐
☐
☐
☐
☐

Fair

☐
☐
☐
☐
☐
☐
☐
☐

You are your own reputation

As a new business owner, you are your own reputation. How you conduct yourself, your premises, and even your outgoing phone message will help to make or break your credibility and your reputation.

Word of mouth is a key factor in a small business's success. You will want to establish a good rapport with your local community. You will NOT achieve this if you are bad-mouthing your competition. Everything you say and do will be judged. You will need to ensure integrity at all times. Be constructive and positive or say nothing. It reflects on you.

Even when you are not at work, you will still need to ensure that you are presenting a good image. Your image is a reflection of your belief in the service that you are going to provide. So is the presentation of your work space. It's very useful to revisit your image and your workspace regularly with a highly critical eye to ensure that you are presenting the image you think you are presenting!

If you are naturally untidy, you may want to keep a treatment room separate from your home – one that has to be kept to a high standard of presentation at all times.

Keep your workspace clutter free. Your aim is to have a calming and tranquil environment and clutter is not conducive to this.

Keep your workspace distraction free. Where possible remove computers, printers, telephones from your treatment area. Where it is not possible to remove them completely, have them behind closed doors or a screen.

Ensure your environment reflects your professionalism. The book case should contain only those books pertinent to your profession – reference books on the subject etc. Your walls should have your professional certificates.

A word about personality – you may have a fantastic personality and wish to share it with all comers. But remember that you are here for your client. It's best to gauge what mood they are in and adapt your personality accordingly. Become a chameleon and reflect yourself back at them to suit their needs. If they arrive full of chatter, then by all means be chatty back. But if they arrive quiet and withdrawn then give them some time and space to be with their own thoughts.

Continuous professional development

Many of the professional organisations recommend continuous professional development and have set up schemes whereby you have to attend a certain number of courses per year to ensure standards are maintained. But as an owner of your own business, continuous professional development is not just about how many courses you've been on. You need to regularly experience the delivery of a treatment that you are offering.

Knowing what it is like to be on the receiving end of your treatment can help you avoid the common pitfalls that growing too familiar with your own treatment can produce.

Reading the latest books on your subject, sharing resources with other like-minded individuals and cross-fertilising ideas between synergistic professionals can all improve your own business.

Feedback

How do you know if you are giving a good service? You know through feedback, of course. Don't be afraid to ask for feedback about your treatment, your treatment room, and yourself and also ask for your client's ideas for improvements.

If you don't ask for feedback, how will you improve?

Feedback can also work well both ways. If you see changes in your clients and they aren't aware of it, then you can either point it out to them or get them to keep a diary, focusing on whatever the change is that you've noticed in them.

Action:
Set up a feedback system and review the feedback you receive.

Discretion

The client is king. They have placed their confidence in you. They deserve your discretion at all times. Do you really need to let their friend know you saw them last week – let alone why? Respect their privacy.

The treatment

The treatment

Diary bookings

Should you use a paper-based diary or an electronic diary? There are pros and cons for both. If you use an electronic diary you can have it internet-based so that your assistant or co-workers or even clients can consult your diary where appropriate. However, if there is a power cut, you've no access to your diary.

I prefer a paper-based diary; when I had an electronic diary in Hawaii the heat of the sun kept causing it to malfunction. It was a nightmare. Each time I couldn't turn it on, I felt I'd lost everything. I hadn't, but it didn't help my stress levels! I've used a paper-based diary ever since.

You will need to keep your appointment diaries for up to seven years in case of tax inspections. I had a tax aspect inquiry last year and was asked to provide details of my itinerary so that my travel expenses could be cross-checked. This was very easy to do as I had kept all my diaries.

Personal safety

If you are a mobile therapist, make sure a trusted person knows where you are, who you are visiting and when you are due back.

If a client is accompanied, you need to think about what to do with them. Will they have access to the rest of your building whilst you are busy with the client? Can you make the other rooms inaccessible?

Some therapists actively discourage additional people and it's not just because of the changed dynamics to the client/therapist relationship.

The Suzy Lamplugh Trust (www.suzylamplugh.org) recommends:

P **Plan** to meet first time visitors in a busy public place, rather than your workplace, if possible.

L **Log** in your visitors with a buddy and phone after to let someone know you are safe.

A **Avoid** situations which could be difficult.

N **Never** assume it won't happen to you.

Before you agree to work alone consult with others who are doing so and your professional organisation - do they have any guidance? Consider how your workplace could be made more secure. Is there some way you can control access to your workplace? Do your own risk assessment and do not let yourself be pressured into working practices that put your safety into danger.

Clients' perspective

Without your clients, you don't have a business. It is essential to keep a client's perspective at all times. Why are they visiting you? What are they expecting? Are you meeting their expectations or exceeding them? Or worse, are you falling far short of what they expect.

Each client is different, so a one-size fits all approach will not work. You need to be different things to different clients.

Your business philosophy should be to see everything from your client's perspective.

When you've been giving your own treatments for some time, you can get jaded. Regularly book in to have a treatment of the ilk that you give yourself.

How are you greeted? What is the room like? What is the experience you are offered? Were you given any after-care advice? How does this measure up to the treatment you currently offer your client? Is there room for you to improve? What worked and what didn't work? Take the learning from your experience with another therapist, back to your own business.

Action:

Set up with a friend that they will allocate someone you don't know to "Mystery Shop" your service. An objective way of checking how well your service is received is to have someone try out your service and report back on their experience, giving constructive criticism.

Between treatments

You may have short gaps between your treatments. Do not get involved in anything else between clients. It's far too easy to get distracted, so that when your next client does arrive, you're not focused on them. How are they? What do they need from you? If you have a few moments between clients, instead, sit and meditate on what works for that client.

Careful who you work with

When sharing a treatment centre, be careful who you agree to work alongside. They can make or break your business for you.

I have had experience of someone stealing from me and the amount of energy that you waste on worrying about how to approach them, tackle the issue, and resolve the problem is valuable energy that you should be focusing on your clients. It's just not worth working with people who have no integrity and if you find yourself in that situation, it's far better to completely remove yourself from the situation and find a new way forward than to battle on, hoping that it will resolve itself. It just is not worth the potential impact on your hard won reputation to put yourself in danger of being tarred with the same brush.

Instead, look for people who are passionate about what they do and who have a positive outlook. You'll bounce off each others' energy and when there is an issue, you'll both be looking for a positive way forward.

Should you sack a client?

In a similar vein – should you ever sack a client?
Unequivocally Yes!

We've all had experiences where we have had clients who are consistently late or who even fail to show up. Whilst I accept that life can get in the way, there are some people who are consistently "no shows". You do not need these people as clients. Each time you keep your diary free for their appointment, they are depriving you of earning your income.

You have several courses of action open to you.
- Ring the morning of the appointment to remind them
- Charge a cancellation fee
- Refuse to rebook
- Collect their treatment fee prior to booking any future appointments

One of my pals charges a cancellation fee but asks that the cheques be made payable to the "Give Youth A Hand" charity so that she herself does not benefit from the fee. She finds it much easier to ask for the cancellation fee when she knows that it is going to a good cause.

I will not ring a client if they miss an appointment. If it is genuine, they will ring back full of apologies, to rebook. If it is not genuine, they do not rebook.

If a client cancels and they are normally reliable you can send a card saying "sorry you had to cancel your recent appointment. It's always good to see you, give me a call to rebook."

I have clients who book all their appointments for the whole year, in January. One is consistently late for every appointment. So I tell her to come on the hour but book her in my diary for a half-hour later. Instead of sacking a consistent client, you may be able to find a compromise that works for both parties.

Giving a client your cancellation policy with their first appointment is a good way of starting as you mean to go on.

Action:
Set up your cancellation policy.

Music licence

During a treatment, you may want to play music for its therapeutic effect. By law under the Copyright, Designs and Patents Act 1988, if you use copyright music in public (i.e. outside of the home) you must first obtain permission from every writer or composer whose music you intend to play.

This means you would have to contact thousands of music creators to obtain their agreement to play their songs in your business or organisation. But to make things easy, the Performing Rights Society (PRS) was set up by songwriters, composers and music publishers to manage these rights on their behalf. So a PRS Music Licence grants you the legal permission to play millions of songs, saving you the time and money needed to gain permission from the music creators directly.

See http://www.mcps-prs-alliance.co.uk/Pages/default.aspx for details.

An alternative is to obtain Copyright-free Music. Copyright-free music is available from a variety of websites including http://www.nvmdigital.com/nvmusic/nvm.html

For my treatments I find any music with a beat tends to cause me to work to that beat. This is known, in drum circles, as entrainment. It can also affect how fast or slow a heart beats. Instead, I choose ambient music with natural sounds such as birds and waterfalls – so that it's relaxing but doesn't affect the treatment untowardly.

Action:
Contact the PRS for a licence or obtain copyright-free music.

Aftercare

Aftercare

After giving a treatment, it is useful to give the client feedback on how well they are responding to treatment. It's also useful to give them aftercare advice. I often give them homework in the form of a list of reflex points to work as a top-up to the treatment.

As it is a holistic treatment you are offering, it's great if you can make part of the solution rest in your client's hands, not just yours. The more you can involve them in their own treatment, the better.

My friend Phil Nuttridge (massagehealth.co.uk) often recommends the "Active Rest Position." His aim is to get the client to focus on relaxing. But if you just say "relax more" will they actually do it? Instead, he demonstrates the "active rest position" and shows them how to position themselves into a way that encourages physical relaxation of the spine and postural muscles. He then tells them to hold this position for 10 to 15 minutes. His clients are told to ensure that there are no distractions in the space where the "exercise"

is to be performed - for example, no television in the corner as this will tend to draw their head and neck in that direction and take away the neutral position of the spine. He also asks them to make sure there are no pets or children around that could jump on them and cause tensing of the abdominal muscles. By doing this and yet focusing on the "anatomy" of the exercise, he effectively ensures the clients create the perfect space for 10 to 15 minutes of pure mental, emotional and physical relaxation

If your aftercare involves a specific exercise, maybe you can have an exercise card prepared, together with your contact information on it and have it laminated. Having something tangible to take away after a treatment will help act as a record of their visit, a useful resource to find your contact details, and can be shown to others – thus helping to increase that all important "word of mouth" advertising.

When advising a client on aftercare exercises, it is useful to link the exercise to an activity that the client does regularly so that they will remember to do it. For example, advise them to do it every time they boil a kettle, or switch on a light.

As part of your aftercare pack, have a feedback form so that you can collect information valuable to your continuous improvement.

Action:
☑ Create an aftercare programme.
☑ Create a feedback system.

Pamper evenings

Pamper evenings

Pamper evening stalls

Pamper evenings or Indulgence evenings are a great way to alert people to your business services. Make sure every local school's parent/teacher association knows your contact details and is aware that you are willing to be involved in any pamper evenings that they may organise.

What are they? They are usually set in a large hall or school hall and outlying classrooms. The public are invited to attend the pamper evening to experience taster treatments of all manner of therapies at a much reduced rate. There are usually also product stalls selling merchandise of an indulgent nature such as jewellery, chocolate, cakes etc. Often the school or charity will have raffles, refreshments, goody bags on arrival to help to raise additional funds over and above the stand fees. They are often staffed by volunteers. Some get very organised and have a programme in which you can advertise your service too.

How they operate: You will be contacted by the organiser and asked to pay a stand fee (average fee in 2008 was £15 plus a donation of a raffle prize). Sometimes the organisers will take pre-bookings so that on the night you will already have a few customers pre-arranged. But on the night you are given a list of timeslots showing which are booked and which are available. You leave this in a prominent place on your stand, with a pen, so that the potential customers can sign their names against an available slot to book their own treatment on the night.

At events where pre-bookings are not taken, you will need a booking sheet for your stand. See example below.

Example of a booking form for a pamper evening:

Reflexology – Jane Sheehan
07739 802175
www.footreading.com

Book your "foot reading" or "reflexology" taster session here

Taster treatments last 15 minutes and cost £15.
Sign your name against a time slot to book your treatment.

Time	Name	Treatment?	Paid?
7.00			
7.20			
7.40			
8.00			
8.20			
8.40			
9.00			
9.20			
9.40			
10.00			
10.20			

Avoid any pamper evenings where the organiser insists on taking all the bookings even on the night. Although it sounds like a good idea, in practice, what happens is that they create a huge bottleneck, and you are left looking at a long line of potential customers who can't come to see you because they are still queuing. It puts off the potential customers and it's totally unnecessary. I wish I'd learned this early in my career!

Also avoid any pamper evenings where they have set the taster treatment rate too low. If you note that the average price for a reflexology treatment in 2008 was £25 for an hour's treatment, then a 20 minute taster treatment should be around £15. (Remember that you will be charging pro-rata with an element for the additional cost of the stand and cost of the raffle donation.) If you set the price too low, then it will be too big a jump from the taster treatment price to the full treatment price and, let's face it, the reason why you are there is to get more long-term customers. Also, if you price it too low, the perceived benefit is lower. There have been times when my friend Sylvia and I have been the only two people charging £15 in a room full of therapists charging £7 to £10 and we've had the longest queues. Don't undervalue yourself or other people will.

Avoid pamper evenings that are organised where there is not already an existing active community. They will be poorly attended.

What is involved in a taster treatment? Exactly as it says. A taster treatment is a way for your potential client to experience a small sample of what you are offering and to give them an idea of what to expect in a full treatment. Practise giving and receiving a taster treatment before the event so that you can check your timings, and check for yourself the experience that your client will receive. That way you can fine-tune the treatment according to what worked and what didn't work for you.

Example of a reflexology taster treatment.

Check that there are no contra-indications (something that indicates that a treatment would be inadvisable). Ask if there is anything specific that they want you to work on. If so, centre your taster treatment on that. If there is nothing specific that they would like you to work on, then focus on

- Spine reflex – each vertebrae represents a different organ in the body so in working the spine you are also helping the whole body, and most people have something which will show up on the spine as being out of balance.
- Toes – in thoroughly working the toes you are helping to relax the mind, the sinuses, the throat, the neck and some of the endocrine system.
- Digestion – do, at least, a once-over of the digestive system.
- With the time left, use relaxation techniques over the top of the foot.

The aim is to leave the client feeling happier and more relaxed than you found them, plus intrigued enough to want to experience more. Do explain what you are doing as you go along. Do ask them to close their eyes and notice what they feel in their body as you are working.

At the end of the taster treatment, open your diary and ask if they'd like to book in for a full treatment next week, explaining the costs. If you don't ask, you don't get. If they agree, write it down both in your diary and on a card for them so that they won't forget and so that they have your contact details in case of cancellation. Make sure you also take their contact information and call the day before to remind them.

Hygiene at pamper evenings

It is impractical and impossible to keep disappearing to go and wash your hands at a pamper evening because of queues, time constraints and distance to the nearest water source. Yet hygiene is of paramount importance.

I use treated wipes to clean the clients' feet and I use a Carex antiseptic wash for my hands between treatments. I also have plasters to cover warts etc.

Paper roll can be used over the couch/chair and replaced between clients.

Advertising the pamper evening

Although the organisers will advertise the pamper evening, do not leave it all up to them. You need to make sure that you make the most of the opportunity, so put up your own poster to advertise the event. Have a copy in your treatment room, your car window, your local café/post office/school/notice-board etc. Tell everyone about it. You're doing them a favour in telling them – who doesn't love a good pamper and an excuse to get out with the girls? Don't be shy!

Once you're at the pamper evening you'll need two more forms of advertising. You'll need a sign to attract people to your stall. It doesn't have to be expensive. I have a poster blu-tacked to two pieces of 3mm thick art board where I've created a hinge with some masking tape on the back. In this way I can stand it up like a birthday card on top of a table. When it's not in use, I use a bulldog clip to keep it shut and as the poster is sandwiched between the art board, it keeps it pristine. In fact, I had the poster professionally made by a graphic designer for the princely sum of £50 including her time, design and the printing of it. The reason that I've used blue-tac to stick it to the art board, is so that when the art board gets all battered, I just have to replace the art board and not the whole thing. Because I also sell my books on my stall, I asked the graphic designer to leave a big space at the bottom of the poster so that the books are not obscuring anything important.

If you can't afford a large poster as described above, you can buy an A4 plastic sign holder from a stationer's for a few pounds, and make an A4 poster yourself with your own computer and printer. Something is better than nothing. Keep within your budget.

Many therapists take business cards with them to these evenings. I have found that because foot reading is so unusual and not many people know what it is, and because I tend to be fully booked up and unable to spend time talking to everyone who passes my stall, a leaflet does a better job for me than a business card.

A leaflet explains at length what it is that you do. Because people are usually hanging around waiting for another treatment booking, they've got time to actually read it whilst they are waiting. If they have any questions, they tend to hover around your stall as a treatment ends. They also have your contact details on the leaflet if they weren't able to catch your attention on the night. It's useful to have your photograph on the leaflet, because as they're seeing many therapists at the event, it will help to jog their memory of who you are, then the next time they see you it will help with the recognition factor.

A word about your photograph:
Don't spoil a good message with a bad photograph. A snapshot will not do. A picture speaks volumes and you want it to be saying a clear business message. You spend a long time thinking about the words you want to say, so why skimp on the photograph? Get a professional shot done, even if it's done by an amateur! Make sure you've had your hair done, your make-up done and you're

wearing appropriate clothes for the image you want to get across. Decide an appropriate location to give the right image. If you can't afford a professional, then consider volunteering to pose for a local photography club provided you can use the shot for your intended purpose. When having a professional shot taken, remember to ask for the copyright so that you can reuse the photograph. It may be worth you putting your requirements in writing in case of dispute about its use at a later date. (See section on Photography Tips)

Equipment at a pamper evening

What equipment you will need at a pamper evening will depend on the service you are offering. Write a checklist of what you will need and keep the checklist to use for each event, that way you won't forget anything. As I do so many, I now have a kit permanently boxed up and ready to take so there is no last minute rush. I have two treatment chairs – one for in my treatment room and one for carrying to events. That way I limit the wear and tear and always have a spare in case of emergency. It's worth investing in washable covers for your treatment chair/couch and a carry case.

Remember to invest in a heavy duty chair/couch. I've had some of the biggest bottoms sit in my chair and I don't want to be worrying about whether the chair can hold their weight. My last chair lasted 7 years and eventually the bolts severed when someone sat in it. So now I will be replacing my chair every six years whether I need to or not. I also check the webbing for damage and replace the webbing as soon as I notice it needs it. No point waiting for it to snap!

Check list for pamper evening

Here is my check list that I use for pamper evenings

- ☐ Table cloth
- ☐ Signs
- ☐ Leaflets and leaflet holders
- ☐ Blank booking forms
- ☐ Pens (leave one with booking form but have spare in case someone walks off with it)
- ☐ Treatment bag. Different treatments will require different contents. I have
  - ☐ Oils (if required)
  - ☐ Foot cream or cornstarch
  - ☐ Antiseptic hand wash
  - ☐ Antiseptic wipes
  - ☐ Plasters (in case of verrucaes etc)
  - ☐ Fairy cards and inspiration cards (for foot reading)
  - ☐ Paper roll
  - ☐ Tissues
- ☐ Merchandise (I sell my own books)
- ☐ Sign showing merchandise pricing
- ☐ Rubbish bag (so I have somewhere to put discarded wipes etc)
- ☐ Money belt with a float of change (better than a box because if it's attached to you it's less likely to tempt thieves)
- ☐ Receipt book if required
- ☐ Treatment chair/couch, stool and yoga block
- ☐ Promotional leaflets
- ☐ Appointments diary (ask for future appointment at end of treatment)
- ☐ Some people take fresh flowers or a bowl of sweets to tempt people to keep coming back!
- ☐ At longer events you may need a flask of drink and a snack.
- ☐ If you're giving a talk then you may need a volunteer to look after your stand whilst you are away from it.

Sample Booking Form for organisers of pamper evenings

Booking Form

Name: ....

Company/organisation (if applicable):......................................

Address: ....

....

....

Tel: ....

Mobile: ....

Email: ....

Website: ....

Products/therapy offered: ....

....

....

Therapists only:-

Please state how long treatments will last: ....

Please confirm that you have relevant insurance: ....

Do you have any special requirements (eg access to electricity/
quiet room etc)...

....

Tables will be either 6ft or 8ft long – state preference ....

My raffle prize donation will be: ....

Please indicate if you require a receipt: Yes/No

Signed:..Date: ....

To secure your place, please return asap to <organiser address>
together with a cheque for £15 per stall payable to '<organiser>'
(raffle prizes will be collected on the night)

Example of a pamper evening invitation

Treat yourself to a great evening out!

<Magazine>, in conjunction with <Venue>,
invite you to an evening of

'Retail Therapy' & Pampering

On Thursday 23rd October, 7pm-10pm
at <address of venue>

*Free admission, lots of shopping and treatments,
complimentary refreshments*
.... bring your friends!

* Shoes * Handbags * Jewellery * Chocolate * Food items * Gorgeous gifts * Foot reader * Cards * Pashminas * Manicures * Beauty treatments * Raffle and lots more

Example of poster for a pamper evening

Treat yourself to a great evening out!

<Magazine>, in conjunction with <Venue>,
invite you to an evening of

'Retail Therapy' & Pampering On Thursday 23rd October, 7pm-10pm

at <address of venue>

Free admission, lots of shopping and treatments, complimentary refreshments .... bring your friends!

* Shoes * Handbags * Jewellery * Chocolate * Food items * Gorgeous gifts * Foot reader * Cards * Pashminas * Manicures * Beauty treatments * Raffle and lots more

for further details see <website>
<charity name> <logo>

Money

Money

There's no avoiding it. Money is one of the main measures in a business. No money, no business.

The first thing to understand is that all the money you earn, is not yours! No! Some of it belongs to the government in the form of Tax and National Insurance payments.

Within three months of starting your business, you must register with HM Revenue and Customs. If you don't, you will incur fines. Their website is www.hmrc.gov.uk and most of the forms you need, plus a beginner's guide is available there for free.

One tip – when registering your business consider carefully how you describe your business. If I call my business "Reflexology" then I can claim for reflexology related books and training. If I call my business "Holistic Therapist" then I can claim for holistic therapy related books and training. (You can not claim for your initial training, but you can claim for courses and books that fall under the category of "continuous professional development"). So you see, it is very important how you describe your business. I had a tax aspect enquiry one year because they wanted to know how a Reflexologist could incur £10,000 in travel expenses in one year. The expenses were genuine, but you can see why it was queried because my business is not similar to most reflexologists. I had to amend how I described my business to suit the change in circumstances.

You don't have to register for VAT until your turnover reaches the tax threshold which at the time of going to print was £64,000. You can check this figure at www.hmrc.gov.uk or by ringing 0845 010 9000

Keep all receipts, bank statements and financial records for at least five years.

> ## Action:
> Register your business with HM Revenue and Customs.
> Ask them for details of available courses.

Banking

It's a good idea to keep your business banking separate from your personal banking so that it's easier to prepare your business accounts. However, shop around carefully before you decide on which bank to use for your business banking. Some charge you per transaction, yet others will offer free banking for an initial period.

"My business bank account charges me for every transaction I make. In order to avoid paying for every transaction, I've set up a Post Office account which does not charge for individual transactions, into which I pay my business cheques. Then I just pay one cheque for the lump sum into my business bank account, thereby paying only one transaction charge yet still benefiting from the business account facilities."
Anonymous

I've done quite a few overseas trips over the last few years with my business and have discovered that it was cheaper to present my foreign cheques to the bank and pay for them to be added to my existing account, rather than set up a separate foreign currency bank account.

It's worth doing your homework. You need to keep your costs to a minimum and your banking charges are no exception to this.

Keep all your bank statements so that you have proof of all your financial transactions in case of tax inspection. Ensure all entries correspond with the equivalent entries in your business accounts.

Cash flow

If you don't get the cash flow right, you could end up out of business very quickly. As a holistic therapist you may be paid mainly in cash and cheques. You tend to get paid after the treatment so it's fairly easy to work out the cash flow in your business. However, you're making the leap, presumably from being paid monthly to being paid per treatment. It gets much harder to budget when you don't know how many treatments you'll be giving or where your next customer is coming from.

Here are some ideas to help you.

Rule 1
Put your cheques in the bank the same day you receive them. Sounds obvious, but you'll be surprised how many people don't do this. Until the cheque is safely in your bank, it is not income. It's just a piece of paper with writing on it. You need that money in your bank as soon as possible so that you can meet your expenditure commitments. Put the person's contact details on the back of the cheque. I've only ever had one cheque refused by the bank but because they'd written their contact info on the back of the cheque I was able to contact them to discuss alternative arrangements.

Set up with your bank a facility that allows you to pay in cheques out of hours.

Rule 2

Offer packages where the customer can buy four treatments at a time. If a client needs four weekly treatments, it's in your interest to have them purchase them in a block to help you establish your income for that month and make it easier to budget.

Rule 3

Chase up all overdue payments. Put a system in place so that you know when your payments are due. As I teach, sometimes I'm paid on the day that I teach and sometimes I have to invoice the organiser and get paid 30 days later. Write down in your diary the date the payment is due and the contact info. Make sure you contact them the week before the payment is due to ask whether they have the invoice and everything they need to ensure timely payment. Ring on the day to ask whether it has been paid. Then ring every day until you know for sure the money has arrived in your account. It's your money, you earned it and for each day it is not in your account, you could be accruing interest charges unnecessarily.

Rule 4

If you find a customer is consistently a late payer, sack them as a customer. You don't need the drain on your energy of worrying about when you'll get paid or if you'll get paid, nor do you need the increase in costs of having to chase it.

Rule 5

If you are planning to expand your business, calculate the impact it will have on your cash flow. Expanding too quickly without proper planning can put you out of business if you have no cash flow to pay suppliers. Consider negotiating staged payments.

Rule 6

Consider having an early bird discount for settling invoices early

What is a cash flow forecast?

When you're running your business you'll want to know what you're expecting to pay out at a later date (Payments) and what money will be coming in to cover those expenses (Receipts) over a given period of time. This is the function of your cash flow forecast and can then be used as a decision-making tool that will allow you to identify:

- How much money you'll need to start up your business
- When you'll need an overdraft or loan
- What level of repayments you can afford
- When you'll be able to spend cash in the future, for example if you want to take on a new employee or pay for a new project
- How much cash your business will be able to pay YOU!
- When cash flow problems may occur as your business grows

When I was considering buying a car it was around the same time I was investing in two new projects. I realised that I needed to learn how to create a cash flow forecast. I had no idea how much I could afford to pay for a car nor how often I could make payments if I took out a loan. In order to broach the subject with a bank I would have to show them a cash flow forecast.

The Cash Flow Forecast consists of three main sections:

- Receipts
- Payments
- Net cash flow/cash in hand

Receipts

In the Receipts section you detail the income the business receives. If you give 30 days credit then anything you invoice today will show up in the receipts section for the following month. If your business is VAT registered then the VAT paid by your customers should be included in the receipts section. (VAT is money you have collected on behalf of HM Revenue and Customs and you need to put it aside and account for it later when you submit your VAT return). You'll also record any other income such as from bank loans, personal investment into the business and bank interest for cash on deposit.

Payments
In the Payments section you detail when you expect to pay your suppliers (so if you agree 30 days credit terms then it would show in the following month). You can sub-divide the Payments section to help you to identify the different costs you have. For example, you may want to record wages separately from rent and utilities or capital investment separately from payments to suppliers.

Net cash flow/cash-in-hand
At the end of each month you take the figure for total receipts and take away the total payments figure.

The net cash flow figure is added to the opening balance to give the closing cash balance at the end of each month. (See example below)

The closing cash balance is the amount of cash your business has available at that given point in time and should correspond with what you expect to see on your bank statement. Where there is a negative figure, you will need to consider alternative sources of funding such as an overdraft facility or an increase in initial investment. (see right)

When preparing your cash flow forecast, you'll need to consider

■ Sales forecast – for a start-up business this will be based on your market research and should be reviewed regularly as you start trading.

■ Credit terms – the length of time your customers take to pay you has a significant impact on your cash flow. You can minimise the impact to some extent by clearly defining your credit policy and by negotiating favourable credit terms with your own suppliers.

Receipts	January	February	March	April	May	June
Cash sales	£2000	£4000	£6000	£7000	£8000	£8000
Credit sales	£0	£8000	£12000	£15000	£18000	£20000
Other income	£10000	£0	£0	£0	£0	£0
Total Receipts	£12000	£12000	£18000	£22000	£26000	£28000
Payments						
Credit purchases	£7000	£9000	£12000	£14000	£16000	£17000
Wages	£3000	£3000	£5000	£5000	£5000	£5000
Office expenses	£2000	£1000	£1000	£1500	£1000	£1000
Finance and tax payments	£0	£500	£500	£650	£650	£650
Capital Expenditure	£3000	£0	£0	£0	£0	£0
Total payments	£15000	£13500	£18500	£21150	£22650	£23650
Net cash flow (Receipts less Payments)	(£3000)	(£1500)	(£500)	£850	£3350	£4350
Opening cash balance	£0	(£3000)	(£4500)	(£5000)	(£4150)	(£800)
Closing cash balance	(£3000)	(£4500)	(£5000)	(£4150)	(£800)	£3550

■ Cash is not the same as profit – if you buy an item at £25 and sell it to a customer for £50 that would be £25 profit. But if the customer doesn't pay you until 60 days later then the business cannot benefit from the sale until the customer pays up.

■ Working capital requirement – in the above example you have paid £25 to your supplier, but you also need to fund the daily costs incurred in running your business and paying for further stock until your customer pays you. If we assume these costs amount to £20 (if only!), you will need a total of £45 to operate the business before your customer pays you. This is the working capital required by your business and equates to the cash needed to fund your day-today operations. When the customer pays you the £50 owed, your closing cash balance is only £5 better than when the transaction first started, even though the gross profit was £25.

Running costs	Income	Profit
£25 + £20 = £45	£50	£5

- Cash cycle – this is the term used to describe the connection between working capital and cash movements in and out of a business. Don't panic – it's easier to understand with an example. Let's say you buy raw materials on one month's credit, and then hold them in stock for one month until you are ready to use them to produce a finished item. It doesn't take you long to make it, but the finished items are typically held for one month before they are sold. Customers then take typically two months to pay for these invoices. Your cash flow cycle would look like this:

	Months	Explanation	Date
Raw material stock turnover period	1	Purchase of raw materials	1 Jan
Less: Credit taken from suppliers	(1)	Payments made to suppliers	1 Feb
Finished goods stock turnover period	1	Issue of materials to production	1 Feb
		Sale of finished goods	1 Mar
Debtors' payment period	2	Receipt of cash from customer	1 May
Cash Cycle	3		

So, in this example, there would be a gap of three months between paying your supplier for the raw materials and receiving cash from your customer. The cash cycle is the period of three months from 1 Feb when the payment is made to suppliers, until 1 May, when cash is received from debtors. This will help you to determine the amount of money you need for working capital. If you can shorten the cash cycle then you can reduce the amount of money you need to fund the working capital.

Setting out your accounts

Contact your local Business Link office or your local tax office to find out when they will be holding their next free course on how to set up your accounts. There is a lot of free help to be found out there and it's best to get it right first time.

When I started, I recorded everything that came in and everything that went out. It wasn't until I had a tax aspect enquiry that I found out that I had been doing something wrong. I had a column for "training" where I included all the income from my giving training courses, and all the expenditure involved in setting up those courses. I also included in that same column the cost of all the courses I attended for my own professional development. What I later found out was that the tax office has certain allowances for your own professional training and really I should have been putting these in separate columns. Despite having paid for an accountant each year, this was not discovered until the tax aspect enquiry. So when I say contact your local tax office for help, I really mean it. Far better to get your accounts set up properly in the first place, than to find out further down the line that you've been doing it incorrectly.

I use an excel spreadsheet for recording my accounts. I record all incoming items and all outgoing items and I put a unique consecutive number on each receipt and record that unique number with the description of the item on my accounts so that I can find it again if I need to.

You will need to discuss with your accountant whether you should pay yourself a mileage allowance, or whether your car should be owned by the business. There are tax implications to consider. You'll need to check the current rates applicable.

Of course, you could also use a standard accountancy software package. Check with your accountant or book-keeper to see what they recommend.

Accountant or book-keeper?

Do you need an accountant or a book-keeper?
A book keeper is someone who does the monthly entry of accounts receivable, accounts payable and, where applicable, payroll. They enter the transactions into the journal, make adjustments and prepare reports. If you're spending an awful lot of your time entering details onto your accounts, then you may consider hiring a book-keeper to do it for you so that you can spend more time earning money.

Once the book-keeping system is set up, someone needs to monitor it and interpret the results. This is the accountant. The accounting process is much less mechanical than the book-keeping process and more subjective. It begins with designing a system that will benefit the business by capturing the financial information in a useful manner without being overly burdensome to the book-keeper. The accountant presents financial statements to the business in such a way that decisions can be made.

I do all my own book-keeping, but I hire an accountant to check my book-keeping annually, prepare my self-assessment returns and my annual business financial statements. I rely on my accountant to guide me on any tax matters and to prepare a forecast.

I learned recently that you can take out insurance via your accountant to cover you in case you have a tax inspection. Tax inspections can take up a lot of time and will cost you quite a bit of money if you need to get your accountant involved. It may be worth your considering this insurance.

Budgeting

When I first started my business I was used to having a regular income from a regular job. I read all I could about how to start a business and time and time again they talked about setting budgets. It really frustrated me. How do you set a budget when you have no idea what you're going to be earning? It's a dilemma.

In the end, I worked it out backwards. I worked out what was the absolute minimum I needed to earn to survive and set that as my target. Obviously, you can't budget if you don't know what you'll earn, but you can at least set targets to help you keep on track.

Don't expect to hit your targets straight away. You're in this for the long haul. You'll need to have some savings put by so that when you miss your targets you'll still be able to pay the bills. That's why a lot of people run their business part-time until they've managed to build up a good number of customers before they take the leap into full self-employment.

Calculate all your outgoings for the year. Mortgage, room rent, utility and phone bills, car tax, petrol, TV licence, hair cuts, food and drink etc. Then find a way to minimise these. Try www.moneysavingexpert.com for ideas on reducing utility bills etc. Now you know your outgoings. Divide your annual figure by 52 to find out your weekly figure and then you know that this is your target minimum income figure for the coming year.

Create a spreadsheet to show the weekly target and each week, type in the actual figure next to the target figure so that you can track how you are achieving. These figures are very useful for you to see annually where your peak earning weeks are and where your worst earning weeks are. You may start to see seasonal trends over the coming years. It's useful to know and anticipate them with either extra marketing and advertising to improve the figures, or by accepting these are the low periods and organising your own holidays to coincide with them.

In year two, you will be in a better position to form a meaningful budget. You will know how much income and how much expenditure you made week on week because you will have recorded it for the previous year. This means you will have an idea of what to expect if all things stay the same. Your aim, of course, is to improve upon these figures year on year. Analyse the existing figures and work out what is working and what isn't working for you.

Don't expect to make a profit in the first year. It's not likely. You'll have one-off start-up costs such as creating your stationery and buying equipment, and you will still be building up your client base.

Profit and loss

The main task of your accounts is to monitor and measure profits, so you'll need to get adept at creating a profit and loss sheet. Don't worry – it's really easy. Your profit is your revenue less your costs.

Record all your income, record all your expenditure and your profit is calculated by taking the expenditure away from the income and

Here is an example of a profit and loss sheet:

	This year	Next year
Revenue	**12,500**	**10,000**
Cost of Sales	7,500	6,000
Gross Profit (Revenue less Cost of Sales)	**5,000**	**4,000**
Gross profit margin (gross profit / revenue)	40%	40%
Operating Costs		
Sales and distribution	1,260	1,010
Finance and administration	570	555
Other overheads	970	895
Depreciation	235	210
Total Operating Costs	3,035	2,670
Operating Profit (gross profit less operating costs)	**1,965**	**1,330**
Operating profit margin (operating profit / revenue)	15.7%	13.3%
Interest	(450)	(475)
Profit before Tax	**1,515**	**855**
Taxation	(455)	(255)
Profit after Tax	**1,060**	**600**
Dividends (A dividend is what you pay out to shareholders or owner)	650	400
Retained Profits (for investment back into the business)	**410**	**200**

seeing what's left. If it's a positive figure, you're in profit. If it's a negative figure, you've made a loss.

When you make a profit, you divide it up into three. One part is what you pay back to the tax authorities. One part is what you pay to yourself (or shareholders if that's how you set up your business) and one part is what you reinvest back into your business to help it to grow for the future.

Once you've created your profit and loss sheet you can use it to compare to future or previous years to see how well you are doing. You can compare it to your plans for the year (did you budget well?) and you can compare it to other businesses. How well are you doing compared to similar businesses? Is there room for improvement?

Keeping costs low

The best tip I can give you in creating a successful business, is to keep your costs as low as possible. When you first start your business, it's very tempting to get carried away spending money on nice stationery, office furniture, new computers, and all the status symbols that you think your business needs. But actually, what your business needs is to succeed. To do this, you need to keep your costs low, and your income higher. When you start out, you can check out websites such as freecycle or ebay and obtain second-hand equipment at a fraction of the cost (or in some cases even for free). Get creative. I met a massage therapist who reinforced a paste-table and upholstered it herself to make a comfortable treatment couch.

Given the amazing range of desktop publishing facilities in standard computers, you can save money on your stationery by having it designed to work with your standard software and printer. You'll note that I still believe in having your stationery designed. It just doesn't have to cost the earth. Another way of having low cost stationery until you can generate enough income, is to purchase a number of the standard leaflets that your professional body produces and put your address on the back. I am a member of the Association of Reflexologists which produces a simple 2 fold "Healing Art of Reflexology" leaflet that explains what reflexology is and what to expect from a treatment. You can get 50 leaflets for £4.50 at the time of going to print.

Your customers are the most important part of your business, so your set-up money should be spent only on things that will attract a new customer, help the customer to have a good experience and to keep them coming back for more. If what you are considering spending does not help with this aim, then should you really be spending it?

If you're very cash poor and time rich, consider swapping skills instead of money. (You will need to invoice in the usual way and show it in your accounts in the usual way, but show that you accepted a service of equivalent value in lieu of payment. If you're VAT registered then you will still have to deal with the VAT payment in the usual way.)

Asking for money

One of the hardest things that new business owners face is asking for their money! I've seen many a therapist quake at the question "How much do I owe you?"

If you can't ask for what you are worth, you won't stay in business for long. Practise asking for the correct payment by watching yourself saying it in a mirror. Practise until it trips off your tongue. Practice asking for more than you initially calculated! See how quickly you get used to saying it!

Notice when you are in shops or having treatments, how do they alert you to the price? Sometimes there's a standard tariff clearly displayed so that you don't need to ask. Sometimes they tell you at the time of booking. Sometimes you just find out when you go to pay. You expect to pay and are not surprised by being asked to pay. So stop making a big deal of it, and start practising how you will ask for payment. It's often not just the client who's mellowed out at the end of the treatment. There have been a few occasions where we've both forgotten about the payment. I've happily waved goodbye to them, then as they're half-way home, I've realised that I've forgotten to charge them. It's best to act straight away, by telephoning them and leaving a message that you've forgotten to charge them, and then let them know how to pay – pop a cheque in the post to you, for example. The longer you leave it, the harder it is to redress the situation.

Start with a price that values yourself and your treatment. It's easy to go from a high price to a lower one, but not the other way round!

Many businesses offer discounts. I don't. I believe in setting a fair price and offering value. To me, when I see a discount, I think that company was overcharging in the first place. If you do discount – remember to inform your customers of the original prices and set a time limit for the discount. Give a reason for the discount. Consider only giving discounts if the client does something in return such as recommending a friend etc.

I've been receiving a newsletter from a therapist. In each newsletter there's news of a discount. To this day, I don't know her full price. What kind of an impression is this giving to her clients and potential clients? Desperation? Over-priced? Value for money?

How much should you charge?

Before you even think about how much you should charge for your services, you need to know a bit more about your customer's evaluation of pricing for services. There are three factors[2] to consider:

1 **Price is a key signal to quality in services**. Consider the last time you went to a Spa for a massage. The perception is that it is a luxury treat and is priced accordingly. But stop and ask yourself whether the treatment was as good as the treatment you've been trained to give.

2 **Monetary price is not the only relevant price to a service customer**. They will also consider waiting time, urgency, physical or psychological cost to them, and reputation. When you are considering how to set your pricing, are you also considering these non-monetary factors?

3 **Customers often have an inaccurate or limited appreciation of the price for services**. When you go to a supermarket, you can often see a wide range of similar products (e.g. juices) displayed in one shelf with price tags so that it is easy to compare these goods. When you are looking at a service, it is not so easy to compare, especially if the services you are interested in are bundled together with other services, thus making it more difficult to compare like for like.

Consider what the customer's reference point will be when they are thinking of what price they expect to pay for your service. It could be the price they last paid for a similar service, the price they paid most frequently, or the price your competitors charge for similar services. It is worth doing a small survey on what price your potential

---

2   According to Services Marketing 5th Edition by Valerie A Zeithaml, Mary Jo Bitner and Dwayne D Gremler. Published by McGraw-Hill

customers expect to pay, a survey of your competitors' pricing and an investigation into the similarities and differences between what you propose to offer and what is already on offer.

There are reasons for the uncertainty of the customer with reference points for services. It's difficult to compare quotes when the services are not exactly the same. The service is intangible. There's often an unwillingness or inability of the provider to estimate prices in advance (e.g. for repair service or for estimating how many treatments will be required for a given condition). Individual customer needs vary. Also, gathering information to create a reference point can be overwhelming for the customer.

I mentioned earlier that there are non-monetary costs involved when considering a service. Customers will trade money for time saved or effort saved or for psychological costs. For example, they'll pay money to avoid the fear of loss (insurance), to avoid the fear of rejection (credit cards at higher rates than bank loans with no questions asked), to avoid the fear of uncertainty (seeing an accredited practitioner rather than an unaccredited practitioner).

There are different approaches to pricing.

First you need to consider the similarities between product pricing and service pricing. All the following are factors that relate to both:

- Demand, costs, competitors' pricing.
- Balancing profit, survival, sales growth, market share, product/quality leadership.
- Price elasticity of demand – the percentage change in quantity bought versus the percentage change in price. (There's a small bandwidth where price makes a difference, too low and there'll be no increase in quantity sold and too high, there are no sales at all.)
- Recovering all costs – direct, indirect, etc.
- Geographic pricing, product-mix pricing (e.g. a printer may be

sold at less than cost price, but the profit is recouped in the sale of the cartridges).

Then consider the three basic price structures and the difficulties associated with their usage for services:

Competition-based price structures
■ Small firms may charge too little to be viable
■ Differences between services offered limits comparability
■ Prices may not reflect the value that the customer places on the service

Demand-based price structures
■ Monetary price must be adjusted to reflect the value of non-monetary costs (as discussed earlier, those of time, effort and psychological cost)
■ Information on service costs are less available to customers, hence an opportunity for the seller

Cost-based price structures
■ Costs are sometimes difficult to trace
■ Labour is more difficult to cost than materials
■ Costs may not equal value

Your price should not be lower than your costs, or higher than what your customer would consider a fair price.

I'm showing you all these different pricing strategies because most therapists go for cost-based pricing, not knowing that there are other options. A big mistake some make when following a cost-based pricing strategy is that they forget to factor in overhead costs. That is, the indirect costs such as heating, lighting, 'phone calls etc.

Action:

☑ Consider each of the pricing strategies and calculate your price accordingly.

☑ It's a good idea to run your prices past your accountant and to review them annually and/or as costs change.

Pricing in a recession

I went to a fantastic talk by V S Mahesh at The University of Buckingham about the pricing of services during a recession. He described a study about retail pricing strategies in recession economies: The case of Taiwan (ref: Chou & Chen, Journal of International Marketing, Vol 12, No 1, 2004, pp82-102). Cut-throat competition caused price destruction. During a recession, many organisations have been destroyed by this. Chou & Chen studied what happened in Taiwan during the last recessionary times there. They identified four types of strategic responses used by different retailers and assessed the relative degrees of success each strategy achieved.

		Organisational Resources	
		Abundant	**Scarce**
Consumer Characteristics	**Less sensitive to price**	Value Strategy	Retreat Strategy
	Sensitive to price	Predatory Strategy	Follower Strategy

Chou & Chen's findings were

■ The strategy that centred on creating value outperformed the other three strategies. That means, increasing the perceived value of what you get for your money rather than adjusting the price.

■ The winners managed to project values that helped move their product/service bundles out of easy comparison with competitors, thus escaping out of straight price comparison.

■ Predatory pricing strategy (undercutting competition) presented mixed effects, with immediate positive effects on sales and market-share growth and negative effects on long-term customer satisfaction and net-profit

    ◆ Customers welcome price cuts but unfortunately they get used to it fast – and resist any attempt to raise prices again when the recession is over. It's easy to go from fee to free but not vice-versa.

I saw an example of this value-centric strategy on 30 July 2008. Starbucks, because they had been forced to close outlets in the US and Australia, decided to announce a free filter coffee promotion. The chain offered a free cup of filter coffee to anyone buying a hot drink and stated that the offer would run for an indefinite period. The perceived value sets them apart from their competitors. This offer was a value-centric strategy involving the 670 outlets in the UK. In fact, the total cost of this strategy was very low because few people take up the offer, preferring the premium drinks.

Action:

☑ Consider how you can add value to your service, without increasing the price, during a recession. Ensure that your service is "branded" so that it is easily recognisable as yours and easily distinguished from others in the market.

☑ Consider how you can package together different services to avoid direct comparisons with competitors.

Another suggested strategy for service pricing is to develop a complete price definition, defining the full range of services that might be required by the customer, then allowing each service to be priced separately, providing the customer a choice of different combinations. Place the highest priced items first in the list.

Consider a strategy where you set a price according to how important the services are to the customer, recognising high costs of failure to deliver the promised service as against the high benefit potential. For example, are you selling a relaxing massage or are you selling freedom from pain? Could you offer two separate services, priced accordingly?

When offering modular pricing, it's best to offer the full premium price first (what you would ideally like the customer to purchase to enjoy the best and fullest experience of your service). Then offer reduced price options formed by putting together fewer modules, thus the customer can see the value and the loss of service per each price reduction.

Speak to any entrepreneur and they will tell you that a recession can also be seen as an opportunity. Not just a problem.

- In a recession, everyone is looking for new solutions to cut costs and improve productivity just to survive.
- Opportunities exist for innovative new services to be launched.
- Opportunities exist for redefining an existing service as a new service by unbundling or by reframing the offer. E.g. reflexology repackaged as an option for stress relief rather than the previously offered option for relaxation.
- Opportunities exist to get customers to outsource their in-company internal services, thus increasing "customer share". E.g. a Spa may hire you on an ad-hoc basis where they would usually hire a permanent member of staff.
- Building stronger relationships by getting through the tough times together.

During a recession

- Look at the other businesses in your sector. What works and what doesn't? Cherry pick the best ideas and make them work for you.

- Look at what happened during a previous recession in your industry. Are there lessons you can learn from then? Are there people still around who can teach you what they learned then? Some industries recover earlier than others so if your industry is one of them, you'll need to know this so that you'll be ready.

- Have any of your competition closed their business? If so, there may be potential clients looking for an alternative solution. When Woolworths closed its doors in my village, I noted how many people mentioned something they wished to buy but couldn't anymore. If I sold those items I could have gained new business.

- Don't stop communicating with your market. During a recession, people may spend less, but when they come out of a recession you want your business to be the first one they call. If you can't afford your usual advertising spend, switch to more lower cost methods such as emailing your client list.

- Cut your costs, not your price. Customers are looking for value so if you increase the perceived value of what you do, you'll keep the customers coming, but it need not cost you more.

Consider whether your product or service is based on a need or a want. When a product is a "need" then the customer is much more likely to quibble over price. When a product is a "want" then the customer tends to find the money to obtain it. A "want" is much less price sensitive.

About value and commitment

I was discussing the issue of value and commitment with my friend Phil. He explained to me that a low price does not always dictate more customers. He gave the example that he runs two exercise classes. They are both the same class, run by him, but one costs £2 per session with no need to pre-book or commit. The second costs £5 with a pre-requisite that they commit to purchasing a terms-worth of sessions at a time. The second class is much fuller and better attended than the first class. The perceived value is higher, despite the higher cost, because of the commitment invested in it.

When and how to put up your prices

Put your prices up annually. The cost of living usually rises each year and as a minimum, your prices should keep in line with the cost of living increases. Most therapists put their prices up in the New Year and this has now become accepted practice.

If you'd like to show your customers a reason for your price increases, you could display the certificates for each course you have attended during the year around your price increase notice. This will indicate how you've continued to invest in your professional development for their benefit. Indeed, should you increase your price after each professional development course you attend?

Put a sign up in your treatment room announcing the date that the price increase will take effect, and write to your existing customers. It's worth offering them a discount voucher against their first treatment at the new price to soften the blow. If you give them enough notice of the price increase, you may even find the number of bookings go up as existing clients try to book in an extra appointment at the old price before it goes up.

If after giving plausible reasons for your price increase, your customer is still querying it, you could always take a leaf out of L'Oreal's advertising campaign – shake your head and say "Why? Because I'm worth it!"

Passive income

When I was preparing to start my own business, I'd attended a few courses and was struck by the idea of creating a "passive income". When you're a therapist you tend to get paid an hourly rate. You give a treatment, you receive a payment. The idea of a passive income is developing a way to get paid even when you're not there. This takes you away from being hourly paid and you can imagine why it would be the holy grail of any business. If you are hourly paid, you worry about taking time out for sickness or holidays. If you develop a passive income, it doesn't matter as much if you aren't able to work every day.

But how was I, a therapist, going to be able to develop a passive income? I decided to write my first book as a way of developing a passive income. I figured that the amount of time it would take to write would be worth the investment if I could sell more than a certain number of copies. It never dawned on me that it might not sell! It was a big risk but I hadn't considered it a risk. When you develop a passive income, I've found that it usually involves taking a big risk. If it works out, it is worth the risk involved.

Other ways of developing a passive income would be to invest some of your profits into other products or services that will yield a passive income. For example, in an ISA, an investment bond or similar. There's always a risk attached to investment, so you have to calculate whether the risk of putting your money there is a risk you are prepared to take. I prefer to invest in things I have some control over, such as writing, producing and selling my own book, or developing my own training sessions.

If you are not able to develop your own passive income, then maybe you could consider cross-selling merchandise to your client base. When selecting merchandise it needs to hold the same perceived values as your service, and be affordable and desirable to your client base. One of my fellow therapists sells Espa products, aligning her therapies with the luxury and quality ideals of the brand. Another sells vitamins, aligning her therapies with the perceived health benefits of the products. Yet another sells Dermalogica products, aligning her therapies with the scientifically researched approach to skincare.

Stock

If you are going to be cross-selling merchandise to your client base, then understand that stock is not income. You need to be careful about your stock levels. You can't sell from an empty shelf, so you need sufficient stock to be able to offer the goods for sale, but you don't want so much stock that it goes out of date, or ties up your capital when it could be earning a higher return on investment elsewhere.

Keep accurate records of your stock levels, taking regular stock checks to become aware of any thefts or any products about to fall out of date. It's better to offer soon-to-be-out-of-date stock at cost price and sell it, than to hold out for the full price and be left with it unsold. Keeping stock in a lockable display cabinet can cut the risk of theft.

A friend had suspected a certain member of staff had been "helping themselves" to the stock. Let's call her Gina.

He valued her other work, but knew he needed to resolve the issue, and quickly.

He called a meeting with all the staff. He explained that stock was going missing and that he suspected outsiders might be responsible. In order to combat this, he stored the stock in a lockable cabinet. The only key for the cabinet was to be held by Gina, who would be responsible for stock records.

It worked a treat. No more stock disappeared.

Negotiate credit terms. Can you obtain the stock on a 30 day credit basis, thus selling it within the 30 day period and paying for it after it has been sold? Can you extend it to 60 days? Can you obtain the stock on a sale-or-return basis?

I'm ashamed to admit that when I produced my first book, I didn't get a selection of quotes for the printing and binding. By the time I produced my second book, I'd rectified this error, and managed to negotiate a much more favourable deal. It's essential that you learn to negotiate. (See chapter on "The Art of Negotiation")

Insurance

When you start your business you will need professional and public liability insurance. You can obtain favourable quotes from your professional body. I am a member of the Association of Reflexologists and the insurance I have with them also covers me internationally.

Consider also obtaining a "wellman" policy (the sort of insurance that will cover you in case of illness).

Other insurances that you may require include

■   insuring your equipment against loss or damage
■   insuring your premises against loss or damage
■   insuring yourself for travel (if, like me, travel is an integral part of your business)
■   car insurance
■   insuring against Tax and VAT enquiries and disputes

With insurance, you get what you pay for. Don't ignore the small print. Get someone else to read and summarise it if you haven't got the time. You don't want to wait until you have to claim on your insurance to find out that you are not properly covered. But don't forget that you can shop around for the same cover.

Do you have a contingency plan? I know a spa which burned down. They had to find alternative arrangements quickly and had lost their appointments schedule in the fire.

A word about holidays

A word about holidays

As a self-employed person, I know how hard it is to allow yourself time out to have a holiday. Sometimes you think you can't afford it, or that your business needs you to be there. I've now changed my way of thinking ever since it was pointed out to me that every time I go on holiday I am so much more efficient the week before I go away!

When I take time out and do something completely non-work related, I often get the most fantastic (and profitable) ideas.

So in effect, there is an opportunity cost of not taking a holiday. If I don't take a holiday I will become more and more inefficient and I won't be getting all those profitable ideas.

When you put it like that, shouldn't we be taking more holidays for the sake of building a profitable business?

A holiday doesn't have to take a lot of time or money. I've been building in mini holidays lasting around an hour! I break my day up into manageable chunks where I have intensely focused work periods, followed by a walk up to the reservoir or a trip to the local café where I meet a fellow therapist for lunch and we inevitably end up bouncing ideas around just by chatting.

Don't sabotage yourself with the boring stuff. If you find you are constantly avoiding doing something, or you find the thought of doing it is draining you, then hire someone else to do it so that you can have a mini holiday from the guilt and worry. Better still, find a way to change your business processes so that you no longer have to do it. Your thoughts become things, so make sure your thoughts are positive and take steps to dismantle anything that doesn't work positively for you. Just because you've always done something that way, doesn't mean you have to continue to do it.

If you're still resisting taking a holiday – imagine what the cost to your business will be if you are ill. To avoid getting ill, you need to ensure you rest and play, as well as work. One of my colleagues takes a one week walking holiday for every 8 weeks of work. He's rarely ill and he's always in demand.

No-one else can resolve your work-life balance. You have to take your own steps to ensure a good work-life balance. Last year I made it my New Year's resolution to gain a better work-life balance. I took my diary and blanked out two days per fortnight for quality "me" time. It makes a big difference to my productivity levels and to my creative ideas. Understand the value of not doing. In this day and age, we're all familiar with "to do" lists. We fill our time up with more and more things to do. But if there were time set aside to do nothing, then we could allow for fresh ideas to come to us. There is power and value in doing nothing. Don't be made to feel guilty about it.

Set boundaries. You need to make it clear to yourself where your work starts and where it finishes. If you work from home, then try putting your laptop away in a cupboard when you are not working – out of sight, out of mind. Make it clear to family and friends what your hours of work and play are, so that they know when a visit would be welcome or inappropriate.

If you are having a day off say "I have no appointments available that day, but I could fit you in the following day" rather than admitting it as a day off. If your services are perceived to be in demand, the client will be pleased that you can fit them in at all.

When you feel your work/life balance is getting out of balance, ask yourself

- What is causing the most stress?
- Is it a temporary thing? In which case, plan accordingly.
- Is it a permanent thing? In which case, seek help.
- What strategies have helped you in the past?
- Can you find a mentor?

Computers

Computers

It's highly likely that you'll incorporate the use of a computer or similar technology into your business. There are a few things I'd recommend you address.

Learn how to back up your information and then set up a daily schedule so that you back up your information. It can be as simple as copying all your important folders onto a memory stick. You may even consider having a series of memory sticks, one for each day of the week, so that you back up Monday's information onto Monday's memory stick, and so on.

Secondly, hire in some technical help. Tim, the guy I hire to build and update my website, also gives me technical support if anything goes wrong with my computer. There was the heart-stopping moment when I was preparing to go on an overseas trip and I was carrying my laptop through to my assistant's desk, forgetting it was still plugged into the printer, the laptop wrenched out of my grip as the cable reached the end of its stretch and the laptop crashed to the floor. It completely damaged the hard drive. I rang Tim up and explained the situation. Whilst I was driving over to his house with a bag full of software and the dead laptop, he was assembling all the things he thought we might need to fix it. A few hours later, he'd changed the hard drive and reloaded the software and we were good to go. Boy, was I glad I'd backed up the computer only minutes before it had happened! I was able to go on my overseas trip, happy in the knowledge that all the presentations were safely restored. I pay Tim a monthly retainer plus the cost of any parts we need. Tim has proved invaluable when I've needed to buy additional technology as he's able to guide me on what I should be purchasing and he's also given advice on how to do things more cheaply by giving me different "work-around" solutions. As my business has grown, Tim's helped me to grow my website and change my technology to adapt to the changing needs of my business.

You could pay a retainer for such help or you could find someone to hire on an ad hoc basis. It would be useful to source your technical help well before you actually need it. There are several companies that will offer such a service.

> ## Action:
> ☑ Consider how you will keep abreast with technology.
> ☑ Plan how you will back up data.
> ☑ Have an emergency plan for technology failure.

Building a website

A long time before I became a holistic therapist, I used to work for an e-business agency. I'd like to share with you some of the things I learned about designing a good website. By that I don't mean that I'm going to teach you how to build the website – I'm not that technical and I bet very few of my readers are either. I am a great believer in hiring in the technical help that you need, but in order to get the most out of the technical help, you have to have a clear idea of what you want and prepare accordingly.

So, the first problem to overcome when designing your website is the idea that a website is faceless. You're going to have to find a way to imply that there are real people behind the website and that if you buy from this website you'll be dealing with honest, reliable and trustworthy people. One way of conveying this is to have lots of photographs of people on your website. Specifically, you should have your own photograph if you ARE your own business. Do not make the mistake of having a family member take a snapshot of you in front of the lounge curtains. It's definitely worth having a professional photograph taken so that the picture also conveys the message that you are a professional. Photographs have what they call "stickiness". People "stick" to a page for longer if it has images, particularly images of people, so illustrate your pages with images of people looking happy (rather than sad).

Ensure that somewhere on your website are your terms and conditions of business. Many small business owners don't give guarantees about their work. Why not? If someone isn't happy with your work, you'd do anything you could to put it right wouldn't you? So why not promise this upfront in your terms and conditions.

What should go on your website? That depends on your aim for the website. Some websites are to give information only. Some are to sell from. Some are for both.

When designing your website, work out what pages you would like. Get a fresh piece of paper for each page that you want to design, and give that page a title. Then jot down what you want to appear on each page, noting the words, the pictures, and the links you'd like to make to other pages.

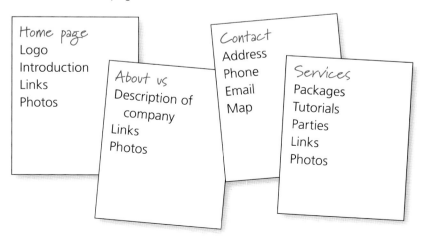

Most basic therapy websites would have:

- Home page (giving a brief introduction about what you are offering)
- About Us (giving details of your qualifications)
- Services (giving details of each of the therapies offered and an idea of cost)
- Contact Us (giving details of how to contact you, where you are located and your opening times)

Each of these pages would have a link to some if not all of the other pages. Remember when designing which pages link to each other that with the latest search technology a person may not be arriving at the front page of your website, so it's important to repeat your key messages on each of the pages and to ensure that they can always link back to your "Home" page and your "Contact Us" page as a minimum.

It's useful to draw the navigation as a flow diagram to help you to understand what you are designing and more easily see if there are any missing links.

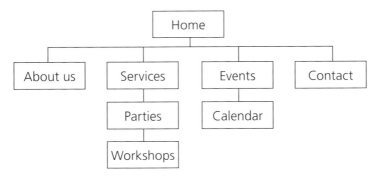

Before you give your website flow chart, and the content (words and pictures) to your website designer, it's useful to have a few objective people look at what you're proposing. When you look at something for too long you stop seeing it properly. A fresh pair of eyes may detect something glaringly obvious that you may miss, such as why not put your phone number on each page?

When considering what to write on each page, remember that you are writing for two different audiences – your human site visitors and the search engine spiders/robots, who trawl the web deciding what each page is about.   In off-line writing, titles are often designed to tease, outrage or intrigue the reader.   But web titles serve a completely different purpose. They serve to tell the search engines what the page is about. So titles need to be clear about what the page is about. Be explicit.

Search engines give extra weight to words in the first few sentences in deciding what the page is about. Put the important stuff first. Ask yourself, "What words would people use as search engine terms to find this page?" then use those words in the first paragraph. In addition, remember that the search engines present their results with a couple of lines summarising what the page is about. These words are often taken from the first part of the page, so they need to be words that will grab people's attention.

Consider typeface – different typefaces can impart personality. Do you want the website to appear **serious**, or playful?   Either way, make sure you could read it easily on screen, so consider what background and foreground colours will aid this. You can set out the list of typefaces used and when they are used, so that if you want to add any future pages you've got a design template to ensure consistency.

It's important to give people a reason to keep returning regularly to your website. If they keep coming back, you can cross-sell to them, make them aware of any changes to your business offerings, and the more they see your messages, the more likely they'll act on them or tell others of your services. You can do this by regularly changing the content, or setting up a newsletter that is sent to the client-base telling them of updates that can be found on the website, or upload special offers at regular (or seasonal) intervals that are available only on your website.

Another way to increase traffic to your website is to set up reciprocal links between your website and synergistic websites. Be very careful when doing this. How good or bad those websites are perceived could have a direct impact on the perception that the viewer will place on your business too. Make sure that they are truly synergistic and have similar values to yours.

You see a lot of newsletters on the internet. Why do you think people create these? It's not just to annoy you! It's a valuable marketing tool. It's a way of increasing traffic to your website. If you can create a newsletter that is informative and useful to the reader, then they will forward it to anyone they feel will benefit from it, so it's good to have a link for people to become a regular subscriber. If it is useful and informative, then it is perceived to add value. If the reader is looking for someone who provides your service, they'll be most likely to come to you first, if you've already captured their imagination on a monthly basis with your newsletter. It helps to establish you as an expert. But it's the content of the newsletter that will make or break this effort.

I keep the content to my newsletter fresh by asking different people to contribute articles and I keep the content different each month, apart from three things. Every issue has a brief news section from me, a horoscope section to give them a reason to open it each month, and a diary dates section that shows when my next workshops, talks, pamper evenings, media interviews and exhibitions will take place. Apart from keeping my clients informed, it's also used by some of my friends to keep up with what I'm doing!

Tips for writing your newsletter:

■ There's no point in writing a newsletter if you have nothing worth saying or worth reading. Understand what you want to impart before you put pen to paper.

■ Pay attention to questions. I wrote my second book *The Foot Reading Coach* because of questions that my students were asking. I am writing this book because now they all seem to be asking about how you start a holistic business. If someone is asking the question and you have some answers, then they're probably worth sharing in your newsletter.

■ Be yourself. If you try writing in someone else's style it will sound wooden. Your passion can only shine through if you're being you! Sharing your own experiences brings a unique flavour to your newsletter that will help to hold your readers' interest.

■ Understand that you can't please all of the people all of the time. You'll always have the odd critic about what you write. Don't take it personally. See if they have a point that is worth considering and learn from that. But don't let it stop you from writing. Remember that for every one critic there are many more supporters. Focus on that instead.

■ Writer's block does not mean that you have no ideas. When writing my second book *The Foot Reading Coach*, I was telling Simon of Human Zoo that I had writer's block. He told me that writer's block is simply having too many ideas that you don't know where to start first. He recommended starting with the most ridiculous first line – a parody of what you want to write, like "Foot Readers are fab" and then continuing to write on from there. You can go back and edit the silliness out later. Just get started. It turns out he was right!

When I first started my website, I had a newsletter, which I manually emailed to 10 email addresses at a time. I'd found that if I sent to more than 10 emails at a time, my server would block the emails thinking that they were spam. Each month it was taking longer and longer to send out the emailed newsletter as my database was growing exponentially. Eventually, I hired an assistant to send the emails on my behalf as it could take a few days to send them out, diverting me from paid work. I saw the newsletter as a valuable way of keeping in touch with my clients and did not want to stop sending it, but I knew I could ill afford to spend so much of my time on it, when the opportunity cost of doing that was too high. After a while, I had a chat with my technical guy, Tim. He investigated using some newsletter mailing software whereby I would create my newsletter, then send it to Tim. Tim would then set up the newsletter to be automatically sent out to the whole of my database using this mailing software. It worked out cheaper per month to pay for the mailing software service than it did to hire my assistant and as the database continued to grow exponentially, the details of each client could automatically be collected, collated and administered to. That freed up my assistant to do other marketing-type work for me. You don't have to put all these technical fixes in at once. Being aware of them means that as your business grows, you can be aware of other options that you can turn to as and when the need arises.

Do you want to sell from your website? On my website we use some software from www.romancart.com which allows us to set up a shop for relatively low cost. You could consider automating the purchase of gift vouchers, or the selling of related merchandise via your website. In this way, you can get the website to start to pay for itself. On my website we sell the books that I have written about foot reading, coaching and holistic business, some related books on shoe reading, the inspiration cards that I use with a reading, my e-learning seminar, and we even experimented with the selling of an e-book written by a friend about her approach to tackling chronic fatigue syndrome.

The great thing about websites is that they yield statistics so you can see how successful your attempts at marketing your site are. You can see the average number of visitors to your site per day, the search strings that they used to find your site and the different countries who are looking at the site. When I appear on radio or TV, I always check my web statistics the following day to see what kind of impact it had. It helps me to understand where my marketing is effective. More recently, I noticed that the search strings were changing and quite a few had been looking for information about six toes. This tells me that I could create an additional page about six toes to help increase the flow of traffic to my site or mention six toes as being part of the content for my workshop.

When naming your website, consider how people will search for it. I decided to call my website footreading.com because it is what someone would search on if looking for foot reading. It's easy to spell. When I'm on the radio, it would be easy for a listener to remember and wouldn't be misheard. Whereas if I chose my own name as the website name it would cut down the traffic to my website (who can spell *Sheehan*? Is it memorable? Can they spell it? Does *Jane* have a "Y" in it or not? etc).

When marketing or advertising via the internet all the usual rules about stating the benefits fly out of the window. Your potential customers are not going to use a search string that will include the benefits. They'll search what it actually is that they are looking for.

When I wrote my first book *Let's Read Our Feet!* no-one could find it on Amazon unless they could remember the full title. With hindsight I wish I'd named it so that a search engine would easily find it if someone was searching on the topic of foot reading or reflexology.

Database

Having a database stored electronically is very useful because it's so much easier to search for relevant information. I know this because for a long time I've been carrying a hefty filofax around with me and it's getting harder and harder to find the names and addresses I need in it, plus I live in fear of losing it! I'm finally investing in a database. I'll need to remember to back up the data so that I don't risk losing all my contacts. But apart from that, it will make life a lot easier.

You could very easily set up a simple database using an excel spreadsheet. A simple database would include set fields for

- First name
- Last name
- Title
- Company name
- Job title
- Address 1
- Address 2
- Town
- County
- Country
- Home Telephone
- Work Telephone
- Mobile
- Email address
- Website

You may also want to add a category field to help you with sorting the database. For example, I have reflexology clients, foot reading clients, seminar organisers and Day 1 seminar attendees and Day 2 seminar attendees, friends and family. I may wish to have a category field that includes a code for each of these types of people so that I can make different marketing messages to each of these business categories and so I can send out party invitations to family and friends only!

I'm about to make major changes to my website because I'll be creating an e-learning seminar. In order to do this, I'll need to change the technology that sits behind my website. I'll need to have a database behind the website so that I can better control the information that appears on the website, change it more easily, and build in better security for access to the e-learning package. Having a database-driven website is more expensive, but worth the investment if you're going to be using the website in a more complex fashion than just an information website.

The art of negotiation

The Art of negotiation

When you start your own business, you're going to have to learn some skills in negotiating. I've never found it easy to do, so I've had to have extra training in how to negotiate to help me to get better at it.

Negotiation isn't about getting the lowest price, but it is about creating win-win situations so that both parties are happy about the deal. This is the best way to build long-term relationships with your customers and suppliers.

To be a good negotiator you will need to exhibit certain common characteristics:

- You need to know what you want out of the deal before entering into the negotiations.
- You need to be shrewd – look for a win-win situation.
- You need to be a good listener – be open to hearing what the other side is looking for and try to accommodate that.
- You need to identify key issues quickly – state what you've understood.
- You need to be creative, patient and seek common ground.
- You need to have empathy for people.

Tip: Don't start negotiating until after there is an agreement to buy! If you start negotiating before a sale is agreed, you waste a lot of time and effort.

Prepare

Before you negotiate, you will need to prepare. Research the costs, the competition, and the profit margins. Have a clear view of the outcomes that are possible – it is worth writing down the worst, best and acceptable outcomes to keep you focused on what you can agree to. Work out at what point it is just not worth making a deal. Plan your exit strategy as much as you plan what you want to negotiate.

When I'm negotiating a corporate team building workshop, I'd want to know in advance

☐ how many people will be on the workshop

☐ where will it be held so that I know if there will be accommodation and travel expenses involved

☐ I'd want to anticipate the hidden costs, such as when I had to complete a one inch thick health and safety document with five appendices which as you can imagine took up a considerable amount of time over and above my usual preparation time

☐ I'd want to know the length of time they've allocated for the workshop, the breaks

☐ whether any other training providers were offering other training modules on the day

☐ I'd also try to find out if the company had done something similar previously, what was involved and what worked and what didn't work from their perspective

☐ I'd also ask for a ballpark figure about what they were expecting to pay. They won't always tell you but it's useful to know

☐ Occasionally, I'll know other consultants who have worked with the company so I'll ring them to ask for advice before quoting. Are they known for paying on time – in which case I don't need to add an amount for extended credit terms etc. (see chapter on cashflow.)

☐ Are there any additional services they might need that I could tender for at the same time?

Preconceptions count

Preconceptions count. The framing of a negotiation can change the game. In an article published in 2000 (in the *Annual Review of Psychology*, Havard Business School Professor Kathleen L. Valley, Senior Research Fellow Max H. Bazerman and their colleagues Jared R. Curhan and Don A. Moore), they mentioned an experiment where it was shown that the amount of cooperation amongst negotiating participants was affected far more by what the game was called – whether the participants were told it was a "community game" or a "Wall Street game" than by the individual dispositions of the participants.

"Simply changing the name of the game changed the mental models the parties brought to the situation, and with it, their perceptions about what was acceptable or appropriate behaviour", the group writes.

Knowing this, how can you "reframe" the negotiation so that you can ensure a more useful mind-set? Think carefully about WHAT you will call the meeting, not just why you are calling it.

The article also outlined that negotiators have a hard time compromising on issues that are sacred to them, and may regard the negotiation itself as immoral. On the flip side, negotiators who declare that a topic is "sacred" and off-limits for discussion - when in fact it is not - can place unnecessary constraints on the game and on their ability to reach compromise.

When you are negotiating, learning what the other party considers ethical or off-limits can be useful. Closing off areas for discussion may affect your ability to reach a solution.

Approach

How are you going to approach the negotiations? Will you have a face-to-face meeting, a meeting conducted over the telephone or will you use email? Each of these methods has their advantages and disadvantages.

If you want to build a rapport, a face-to-face meeting is best although it will cost you more in time and money to set up, once you've factored in travel time too. Generally face-to-face meetings allow you to foster rapport and also present fewer opportunities for misunderstanding or deceit. If both parties are already familiar with each other, however, face-to-face meetings may not be necessary. And if tensions are already high, then negotiating by phone may be the best choice, to reduce the possibility of pressure tactics.

Since e-mail lacks what researchers call social context cues, it allows more "talk time" for all, and this dimension of egalitarianism may make for a more fruitful exchange. There is a downside, though, because e-mail also seems to make people less inhibited in a negotiation scenario. If the negotiation is already tense, this lack of inhibition can make a bad situation worse. (One study found, for example, that among 24 four-person decision making groups interacting *via computer*, there were 102 instances of rude or impulsive behaviour. Yet the 24 four-person decision making groups that interacted *in person* yielded only 12 remarks of that nature.)

Before arranging your meeting, given the above pros and cons, decide which format will work best in your situation face-to-face, email or telephone.

Find Common Ground

Find some common ground first before launching into negotiations. Professor Daniel L Shapiro, associate director of the Havard Negotiation Project, has identified **five core concerns** as critical in creating disputes and finding resolution.

- **Autonomy** – a person's freedom to make decisions for himself
- **Appreciation** – having actions acknowledged
- **Affiliation** – being treated as a colleague
- **Status** – feeling others respect one's standing
- **Fulfilment** – having roles or activities that are fulfilling

Cross one of the core concerns above and conflict arises. Respect them, and compromise is round the corner.

Be Nice

It sounds obvious, but "be nice". Never allow your ego to negotiate! People respond well to people who are calm, friendly and nice, but will want to hurt the jerk! Start off on the right foot! They may decide to be brusque, unhelpful or worse. Don't let their style distract you. Keep restating your priorities and your goals calmly.

What do They Want?

Don't assume that you both want the same things from the negotiations. (Assume amkes an 'Ass' out of 'U' and 'Me'!) You'll have put in a lot of preparation about what you want out of the deal, but there's no point even beginning to discuss your wants until you find out what they're looking for. Begin by saying "I'd like to talk about an issue that's important to me, but before we start, I'd really like to hear what you have to say." Then really listen to what they want out of the situation. What are their hopes and their concerns? You're looking to find areas of common ground, where you can reach a mutually beneficial agreement. You're not looking to win at all costs. If you make someone else cave in on an issue that is really important to them, you will ruin your long-term relationship with them. Instead, you're looking to find a mutually acceptable compromise. Always let the other person save face.

Listen

Listening is one of the biggest skills required for good negotiations. If you aren't able to listen out for what the other party wants, you're in no position to even begin to offer them a solution. Some people go into negotiations thinking that the resources are limited and that they want the biggest slice of the action. But, not everyone wants the same thing out of a deal. And because of these differences, a deal can be reached where both parties can be happy with the solution.

Take buying a new car for your business, for example. Usually, the dealer wants a sale and to make a profit. Yet, don't assume you know what they want. If business is slow, the dealer may have a cash flow problem and be willing to settle for less or even for no profit, in order to generate cash. You, on the other hand, want a vehicle for your business. Factors that affect you apart from price are style (what does the car say about your business and can you fit your advertising on it?), ease of maintenance, reliability, warranty, miles to the gallon and other factors that the dealer doesn't really care about.

The art of negotiation is to find the common ground on which a deal can be made.

One Item at a Time

Concentrate on negotiating one aspect of the deal at a time. Don't give them too many options to consider at once. You don't want to lose the opportunity to arrive at an agreement by making it too complicated.

"If ... then" Statements

When negotiating, tell them what you'd like them to concede, before you tell them what you'll do in return. Consider this statement:

■ If you book four treatments at weekly intervals, I'll give you a 10% discount.

By beginning with the word "If", the listener knows there are two parts to the story and when you begin with what you want from them first then they are more likely to continue listening to hear the clincher. It's always better to have something to offer the other person rather than just them having something you want.

Reversing the order makes the offer less strong:

■ If I give you a 10% discount, will you book four treatments at weekly intervals?

They will expect the 10% discount to be there even if they don't fulfil their part of the bargain.

Give-aways

Don't give anything away if it isn't exchanged for something else. There are things that might be of high value to one party but low value to another – these are great bargaining tools. I can give something away that is low value to me but high value to my client in exchange for something that is low value to them but high value to me. E.g. paying a deposit up front may make no difference to a large corporation, yet covers all my costs and allows me to not worry about the slow payment that may only arrive after my credit card bill is due.

Prioritise - what is essential for you and what could you "give away" if you need to shift to get to an agreement? Don't give away your essentials lightly!

Try and find out or work out what is important to the other party and use that to help shape a deal.

Set Expectations

Starting out with high expectations, means that you're more likely to have a good outcome. It's a self-fulfilling prophecy: what we expect tends to come true. Don't believe me? In a famous report (*Rosenthal & Jacobson, 1968*), Rosenthal describes a case in which a researcher told teachers that a testing program had identified some students as having high potential and others as having low potential. In fact, students had been picked randomly and assigned to one of the two groups. The results after a year in school showed that the so-called high potential group showed significant gains in achievement and ability as measured by standardised tests.

Rosenthal's initial report has been followed by twenty years of research exploring the limits of the self-fulfilling prophecy. The thinking today is that we can influence our level of performance and that of others by the level of our expectations.

Be Consistent

What's known as the Pygmalion Syndrome also comes into play here. (According to the myth, Pygmalion created a female statue and treated it with such affection that, through Aphrodite's intervention, the statue came to life and responded to him). If you look like me and act like me, or like I think you should, then you are predictable and that makes me feel better because I know how you will react to things and I can manage the outcome. This is a common psychological factor, so knowing this when negotiating, you can change your approach to mirror the other party's or you can act consistently so that they are secure in the knowledge that they know how you will react.

Repeat your Understanding

Define clearly what you want. If you negotiate a deal and both sides think that they are negotiating for something different then you won't have been successful. To avoid this happening, repeat regularly what understandings you have reached. Ideally you want to build a relationship where "Yes" is the most said word. One of the most important skills of a negotiator is summarising – it confirms common ground and invites the "Yes". Top negotiators summarise what's been said up to four times more than their counterparts.

Illigoical Leaps

Beware of people who get you to agree a few things then make an illogical leap.

Q: Do you want to save money?

A: Yes

Q: Do you want convenience?

A: Yes

Q: So you'll want to sign this 12 year commitment then?

A: Yes. What? No way!

Silence is your Friend

Use silence and the word "No" a lot! Don't feel you need to talk the most – you often give things away without meaning to. Don't be afraid of disagreeing – sometimes you need to walk away and come back together after a break. Conflict is inevitable in some scenarios so accept that it may happen. Remember that you are not a charity – you need to make money on everything you do or have the potential to make money. Keep coming back to percentages.

Don't name a price first. Gain an idea of how much the other party is offering or expecting.

Never accept the first offer. It's probably not their best offer.

Facial Expressions

Use your facial expressions. I found this technique out by accident in Thailand. My friend, San, and I were negotiating a price for a colourful quilt. They gave me a price, so I turned to San and in Malay I said "is that too dear or is it cheap?" San, struggling to translate my Malay, screwed up her face in concentration. At this, the trader kept bringing the price down. The more San looked disgruntled, the more the trader dropped the price. Result!

Timing

The person who has the most time is likely to get the better deal. If you have a tight deadline, the other party can wait until you have to act. You feel pressure, whilst they feel calm, collected and patient.

You can take advantage of this in your own negotiations by setting a time frame for the offer. You'll have heard similar tactics on TV ads that say "Buy now whilst stocks last." You offer treatments at a discount for a limited period, or add an additional item or service in with the price for a limited period. Where something is considered in scarce supply or on offer for a restricted period, there's a much stronger urge to act on the offer than if it is perceived to always be available.

Information

The more information you have, the better the deal you can negotiate. If you are aware of competitor rates then you are able to mention these in your negotiations.

Take advice. Experiments have indicated that negotiating teams have distinct advantages over negotiating individuals through an enhanced ability to exchange information to generate high quality ideas.

Avoid Automatic Contract Renewals

My colleague was looking at her annual phone bill. She rang the company to say "I'm looking at sorting out my package. There are a lot of offers around and I'm coming to you first." It turned out they even had a customer retention department and put her through to them. They reduced the bill by £10 a month without even tying her to a contract.

Flushed with the success of this, she then tackled her annual renewal of buildings and contents insurance and reduced the bill by £100 by reapplying online instead of allowing the automatic renewal of it.

It also helps to have a good idea of what the other party wants and what their priorities are.

For example, if a client is coming to you for a therapy as a preventative measure, you'd present a different offer than if they were coming to you for a specific health issue. Similarly, you'd want to establish if they'd be having a treatment weekly, monthly or on an ad-hoc basis and may alter your pricing accordingly.

Breaking down the level of services offered into modules

When deciding what to negotiate, it's useful to set out the number of services offered as modules. If there is a negotiation based on price and they are unhappy with the price level, then you have the option of reducing the number of services offered in order to arrive at their price level. Or to increase the number of additional services offered yet keep the same price so that the perceived value of the contract is higher in the eyes of the other party. If you'd prepared your price structure in a modular manner then this would be easier to calculate by both parties.

Exceed Expectations

My good friend Alice, who has owned both a hair and beauty business and a restaurant, says that in business it's best to underpromise and overdeliver. Surpassing the expectations of a customer is a sure-fire way of retaining them.

Getting to No

If you never hear "No" when you are negotiating, you've not asked for enough!

Don't be afraid of hearing "No". It's all part of the art of negotiating. You've found the ceiling of what they're prepared to deal. Knowing the boundaries is extremely useful.

When you hit "No", it's really time to listen. Ask if they mind explaining the reasons behind why they say no. Through listening you can find some common ground. Stay calm, don't yell and don't walk away. Perhaps you can ask for some time to think through what they've just said and come back to them with some ideas at another meeting. In this way, you can re-evaluate your proposition, taking into account any areas of common ground and taking into account any motivating factors that you've discovered through what they've revealed.

Planning your exit strategy

Always keep your options open. Have a fallback position. Always know when to fold. Know your bottom line and be prepared to stick to it.

Be brief. State your case factually but without using words like "I disagree" as this will automatically throw the other person into defensive mode.

Avoid empty threats. They diminish the other person's respect for you.

Avoid surrendering on important issues or forcing the other person to cave in on issues important to them as this will damage any long-term relationship. Instead, focus on finding a compromise rather than an outright yield.

Never walk away from a deal with a "take it or leave it" ultimatum. Always leave room for re-opening talks. Try "it looks as though we can't agree today. Let's sleep on it and talk later".

My parents still have a letter from my brother (then 11 or 12 years old) when he wanted to go to school (on the other side of town) on his bike. Obviously, his initial negotiations must have failed, so he wrote an impassioned plea to be allowed to use his bike, laying out all the health benefits of open air and exercise versus stuffy bus, his qualifications e.g. he knew his highway code, fewer fights and squabbles on the way to and from school, a promise to wear hat and gloves, his method for safely transporting his school books. I don't think his objection to having to relinquish his seat to "old biddies" on the bus strengthened his case, but I think that he won the negotiation! He now (30 years later) runs a successful business of his own!

Action:

Practise your negotiation skills regularly. With practice you can improve your skills and become more confident.

Negotiating check list

- ☐ Is there an interest to buy?
- ☐ Have you prepared your facts?
- ☐ Have you set their expectations about the meeting?
- ☐ Have you decided upon the best approach?
- ☐ Have you acknowledged the five core concerns? (refer to section on 'Find common ground')
- ☐ Have you discovered what they want from the negotiation?
- ☐ Have you repeated your understanding of what you both want?
- ☐ Do you both understand the required timing?
- ☐ Have you broken down your deal into modules?
- ☐ Have you planned your exit strategy?

Tough times

Tough times

All businesses face difficult times at some stage in their life cycle.

When the going gets tough, innovate. Creating new products, services, and marketing programs is a strategic necessity. Holistic Business can often launch new ideas without large capital investment, making the risk of a single investment going wrong quite manageable.

■ Seek opportunities to grow your market or repackage your services to reach new markets. Could you join in networking events organised by your local Chamber of Commerce or Federation of Small Businesses? *See the chapter on networking for further details.*

■ Don't loose sleep. Always get a good night's sleep so you are fresh and can save your waking hours for clarity and creativity.

■ Meet with other business owners to bounce ideas, cross-fertilise ideas and perhaps you'll see a new way forward or even create a new service together. If their business is in a completely different sector to yours, they may have a common business practice that could work in your sector but that no-one has thought of doing.

For example – in the car industry it's common to give you a trade-in price for your car. One computer company owner, after bouncing ideas with a car dealership owner, decided that it just might work in his sector too and started offering a trade-in price for replacing a customer's network.

■ Meet with business owners who offer services that are complementary to your own. There may be some way that you can support each other.

For example – in my reflexology practice I'm a great believer in empowering the customer to help themselves. I don't see reflexology as an alternative approach in that it is not a cure-all, but I do see it as a complementary approach to other forms of medicine and therapy and when working with clients I will do my best to help them see the more holistic picture concerning their health. If there's an exercise regime that I think will help prevent them from their recurring back pain then I'll allocate it as homework. If a client has coeliac disease, then I recommend a local herbalist. In return, if the herbalist or the trainer has clients who they think would benefit from my approach then they will recommend my services.

- **Innovate.** It could be through a new marketing approach, a new way of promoting your service, or putting together your existing services in a different way.
- **Consider a different business model.** For example, if you've always sold products in your treatment room, could you set up an on-line outlet for selling these products?
- **Be ruthless in assessing your business** – some areas of low profit may be absorbing all your time and resources when other areas of high profitability may be being neglected.
- **Understand why your business is having problems.** Sometimes you may need a fresh set of eyes to help you to see the bigger picture – warts and all. There may be free advice available from your local **Business Link** or **Small Business Development Centre.** Maybe you know someone who has been through a similar experience and would be willing to share their experience and advice with you.

- **Don't be afraid or too proud to ask for help.** There are always a number of generous people with experience and advice to set you off on the right path. Don't reinvent the wheel. People have been down your path or a similar path.

- **Bite the bullet no matter how painful.** If it looks as though you have to shut down an area of your business, or declare yourself bankrupt, it's better to bite the bullet and tackle the situation sooner rather than later.

Sometimes you make business mistakes. The important thing is to learn what works and what doesn't work so that you can move forward and avoid repeating the same errors. Don't beat yourself up. It's not useful. Instead make the experience work for you. Mine the experience to glean the learning from it.

A few years ago I hired a theatre to put on a show called "You Revealed" in which a team of us put on an edutainment event aimed at showing the audience different aspects of themselves through analysing their body, home, aspirations and astrology. We broke even but we did not make a profit.

The idea was a good one, but the execution of it could have been better. After the event, I analysed what worked and what didn't work and wondered how it could be done differently to allow a more profitable outcome.

- Understand the core market properly – we aimed efforts at the general public when it was mainly therapists who attended.
- We were advised by the theatre that ticket sales improved if a free glass of wine upon arrival was offered as part of the deal. A similar promotional idea with a freebee more targetted to therapists may be worth considering next time.
- Replicating the efforts over several theatres in several areas, setting up a tour, would mean that the overall costs could be reduced through economies of scale, and a momentum could be produced through word of mouth if the geographical area was not too great between theatres.
- Replicating the efforts over several theatres would also mean that different promotional offers could be tested.
- Selecting a theatre nearer to the performers' home-bases would mean a better understanding of the local area, market, and advertising opportunities and would cut down on travel and accommodation expenses.

Another example of how you can learn from business hiccups, if you remember not to spend too much time beating yourself up over it, was related to me by a holistic therapist. Let's call him Adrian.

Adrian had qualified as a sports and remedial massage therapist and had been steadily growing his client base over a number of months. He practised from a treatment room at the back of his home which had all the benefits and conveniences one would expect from that. Adrian however had a belief, which later proved to be a "limiting" belief, that by only practising from home he was placing a number of restrictions on the growth of his business. There were three aspects to this belief.

First of all he believed that a number of potential clients would be put off coming to his home for treatment - the *male-masseur-luring-female-clients-to-his-home* syndrome!

Secondly he believed that a business based from home would be seen as a second-rate business whereas a business based in a therapy centre would be seen as more clinical and professional.

Finally, he believed that in order for his business to reach its full potential he would need to tap into the passing-trade market that would only be available through working in a high-street-based clinic or therapy centre.

Adrian then heard of an interesting opportunity. A therapist, let's call her Jaz, had taken out a lease for premises in the centre of his local town. These premises were very promising as they offered the potential for four treatment rooms and a reception/waiting room area. Jaz was looking for synergistic therapists who would hire the spare rooms from her with a view to setting up a therapy centre. Adrian met with the other people who were considering renting the other rooms and they seemed like a nice bunch. Indeed he knew a couple of them already and thought that if they considered it a viable proposition, then it must be! (He later discovered that these friends of his, on seeing him at the meeting, arrived at the same conclusion and used that as the basis of their decision making too!) Adrian could see himself happily working alongside them and the location and set-up of the centre nicely appealed to each of his three limiting beliefs. Adrian and the others duly signed a contract with Jaz to take a treatment room each for two years. Adrian even offered to cover a good proportion of the deposit required by the landlord to secure the premises.

Initially, all seemed to be going well. But within a couple of months Adrian found out that Jaz had fallen into arrears with the rent payments to the landlord. He and his fellow therapists had been paying Jaz their proportions of the rent but that wasn't enough to meet the whole rent burden; he also discovered that Jaz had pre-existing debts and was being pursued by a previous landlord for other unpaid rent! To cut a long story short, the centre folded and deposits were lost. Fortunately only Jaz's name was on the lease with the landlord, so no one other than Jaz would be pursued for unpaid rent.

Adrian had lost the sizeable deposit he had paid and ended up with a room full of furniture and nowhere to put it (he had kept his treatment room at home even when the centre had opened, so he had purchased a new treatment couch, desk and so on for the therapy centre). Adrian now had no choice but to return the focus of his business to the treatment room at his home.

It would have been very easy to become bitter about the experience, and as Adrian later admitted there were times in the early days when he did feel a huge amount of anger. However, Adrian soon realised that the whole episode actually had become a very valuable learning experience. Once he was back home working, his business actually grew by leaps and bounds. Life was simpler as he no longer juggled a diary of some treatments at home, some at the therapy centre. His clients also no longer had to find town car parks before a treatment – they simply parked on his driveway. Female clients came to his house without problem; Adrian realised that his main route for new clients was "word of mouth" and hence any new clients who came to him already knew an existing client and they would allay any fears the new client may have over visiting a male therapist's home. Adrian also realised that he had gained very few "passing trade" clients whilst at the centre. As for his fear that treatments at home would not be seen as sufficiently professional, the constant stream of clients to his front door proved that to be a myth too.

The therapy centre experience had allowed Adrian to explore his limiting belief and had very nicely demonstrated it indeed to be a limiting belief. Although he had lost his deposit, the fact that the centre folded within a few months meant that Adrian had sufficient time to learn from the experience but wasn't then burdened with continuing rent for the remainder of the two-year lease. When I asked Adrian whether the experience was a bad experience he adamantly replied "no – it was money well spent because of what I learned about my own business and my limiting beliefs. Because of the experience I would say my business has grown bigger and better!"

Displacement behaviour

When you've been in business for yourself you can fall into some bad habits. One of mine is procrastinating! I'm worse when I'm writing a book. As I approach the computer to start writing, I suddenly remember all the things I've been meaning to do (or really avoiding doing because there's something more interesting to do). I put the clothes washing on, I mop the floor, I polish my shoes – all those things that stop me from actually doing what I'd planned to do! That's what I call displacement behaviour. It's displacing me from doing what I need to be doing. It's crazy, but I know I'm not the only one. I speak to other business owners and I find that they do it too. I decided that it would be worth investigating how to tackle such behaviour.

- ■ Firstly, look closely at how you procrastinate. Are you surfing the web, checking your emails or, like me, are you doing all those household jobs instead of getting on with what you're meant to be doing? Once you learn what you do to put off what needs doing, it's easy to work out a strategy to eliminate that behaviour. If you can't eliminate it, then at least save it as a reward for after you've got the job done.

- ■ Keep a day planner. Write down what has to be done (a "to do" today list) and then block out time in your planner to allocate each of these jobs. Once you've done it, tick it. You get a great sense of achievement when you can look down the list and see all those ticks. It will motivate you to move onto the next task.

- ■ If you don't absolutely have to do something, don't put it on your "to do" list. Adding tasks you don't have to do will make your list so long that it will feel overwhelming. Better to just focus on the important stuff. I worked for a guy who used to split a sheet of paper into 4 with the headings "Important and urgent", "Important but not urgent", "Urgent but not important," "Not important and not urgent". He tackled the Important and urgent column first and then the Important but not urgent column second and if he had any time left he'd do the other columns. I learned from him that just because someone else has a crisis and a rush on, it doesn't mean that it's your priority.

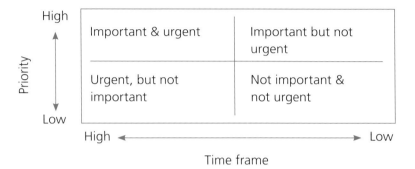

If you are procrastinating because you really think it doesn't need to be done, then don't waste any more energy procrastinating over it. Make a decision that it doesn't have to be done and cross it off your list completely.

I have a bit of a butterfly brain. I often think laterally and get great ideas about something else when I'm in the middle of an important project that I have to finish. I have a huge A1 sized white board near where I work. I use this to keep track of my ideas so that, if I have an idea in the middle of doing something else, I can park it on the white board so it can be addressed at a later time. It works well too for all those interrupting phone calls – I write the action requested on the white board and get back to my original task. (Maybe I should let the answer phone get the call!)

Substitute a less daunting task than the one you are putting off. Make sure it accomplishes the same thing. Instead of writing a letter, can you send a postcard?

When I was faced with writing this book, it felt like such a big topic and where do you start? How I began was to brainstorm topics with a friend. Then rather than think of writing the whole book, I started to select just one topic off the list and write about that. If I was asked to write an article for a magazine, I'd select one of the topics and write it for use as both the magazine article and a chapter of the book. In that way, it made writing the book less daunting.

- At the end of the day, write down what you've accomplished. This can be its own reward.

- Check email only when you have time to answer any new messages. That way you are looking at them only once.

- If you are procrastinating because you really don't like the task you have to do, consider whether someone else could do it for you. Why do you think so many people hire cleaning ladies!

- Write down a set of goals for the day, the week, the month or even the year. Look at how your procrastination is preventing you from reaching these goals.

- Do it tomorrow!

Last night, I'd left everything I needed to get done today on a list on my bedside table. Whilst I was drinking my first cup of tea this morning, I reviewed the list and determined that I'd do everything on that list first, before I got sucked into the usual daily routine. Terrific. I got everything I needed to get done first, and somehow it was easier to start because I'd predetermined the day before what I should be doing that day.

There's a time management guy who advocates "Do it tomorrow". I guess in the light of this experience, he could be right! Or am I just procrastinating again?!

■ At the end of your day, if you've achieved what you set out to do, reward yourself in whatever way you see fit. Having an incentive to finish is more likely to get you to do it!

■ Tell someone what you're going to achieve today. I have a friend who I tell what I'm going to do, and then I know they'll ask me tomorrow if I managed to do it. If you know someone's going to check up on you, it's quite a motivator.

■ Break a big task down into measurable chunks. For example, if you have to deliver 2,000 leaflets, break them up into 100 leaflet batches and reward yourself after each batch.

■ Just do it! The most difficult part of any chore is getting round to starting it! Make it easy to start. Once you begin, the task is even easier than you expected. And when you have completed it, the feeling is fantastic. Stop procrastinating and take the first step NOW!

■ Eat a frog for breakfast! I went to an Action Coach seminar where they asked if you have to eat two frogs for breakfast and one is really cute and good looking and the other is ugly and warty, which would you eat first?

If you started with the ugly one first, it would be easier to continue to the second one.

So when you have a list of tasks to do, start with the worst one so that the day just gets better and better!

Beating isolation

Sometimes working on your own all day every day can feel rather isolating. I love my own company, but even I get fed up with being on my own sometimes.

This year I decided to set aside some time where I'd invite a friend over so that we could work together. By that I mean we'd bring our laptops, phones, and a project, and we'd work separately on our own businesses, but do it together in the same place. I'd save my least favourite jobs to do at that time. There's something about having other people working around you that generates a buzz that you can't feel on your own. All of a sudden, those least favourite jobs suddenly seem so much easier to tackle. You can see that they are working, and you've set aside a finite time in which to do them and you get cracking.

At a network event, we mentioned it to another friend, and she said she wished she could do something like that, so we invited her to our next one. It's now a regular fixture in our working calendar. The best bit about it is, after two hours of solid work, we put our work away and have coffee and cake together before we go our separate ways.

If you're going to do this, you have to set some ground rules.

- Set a start and finish time
- Be punctual
- Set 15 minutes at the start to have a few pleasantries and a catch-up (we use an alarm clock) and when the time's up, get to work!
- Everyone knows where the coffee and tea is kept and if they want one, they have to make everyone else one. No interrupting the concentration by asking if we want one. If we don't we just won't drink it.
- If anyone wants to bounce ideas, then we pre-agree a time.

Bailing out – knowing when to quit

Sole traders who run into business troubles often go through the same processes that dying people do: denial, anger, depression and then finally acceptance. The sooner you face up to the problems, the better. The aim is to minimise the losses, try to turn around the situation, or if it's untenable, then to close the business before you sustain too large a loss.

Keeping a close watch on your financial data should be a priority. Simply put, if your expenses are consistently higher than your income, then your business is not sustainable.

What are the warning signs?

Financial:
- Declining income and/or profit.
- Having to juggle to be able to pay the bills.
- Sustained losses, especially for more than 12 months.

■ Substantial debts.

■ Suppliers requiring cash on delivery or cash in advance.

■ Inability to forecast performance.

■ Fatigue in customer or supplier relationship.

Operational:

■ Repeat concerns.

■ Too much money tied up in stock.

■ Poor delivery performance.

■ Tired looking customer areas.

■ High employee turnover.

■ Management defensiveness.

Look at your appointments diary regularly. You start to get a feel for the ebb and flow of custom. You'll better be able to anticipate the threshold of when it's too quiet or too busy. If you spot a quiet time, you can try to turn the situation around through marketing, advertising or a special promotion.

Keep an eye on your prices versus costs ratio. Many therapists are shy about increasing their prices, worrying that they'll lose their custom if they do. But if your costs are rising, then it's essential that your prices reflect this.

Above all, don't bury your head in the sand. If you are losing money, losing customers and losing sleep over your business, then ignoring it won't make it go away.

Working abroad

Working abroad

The original title of this book was going to be "Business from a Backpack" but I realised that very few of my contemporaries actually work abroad!

Preparation is the key to working abroad. I've worked in United States of America, United Arab Emirates and Australia, sometimes through invitation and sometimes because I set it up myself.

If you're thinking of setting up your own work in another country, then I've a few tips based on my own experience.

■ Investigate the entry requirements such as visas and the rules around working in that country.

■ Investigate the market.

> When I went to Australia the first time, whilst I did some research into the areas I wanted to work, I hadn't realised that whilst in Britain there's a population of around 55 million people in such a small geographical area, in Australia there are only around 20 million in a vast geographical area. Consequently, I shouldn't have expected my workshop attendance figures to be the same!

■ Investigate the climate. Will you need hot weather gear or cold weather gear? Don't assume that your usual clothing will be appropriate for the climate.

I'd been warned that it would be similar to a UK spring when I visited Australia in winter. I packed accordingly. However, in the UK, when you see sunshine it means it's warm. So each morning I'd look out of the window, see the sunshine and set off in a t-shirt, only to return a few seconds later to grab my coat! In Australia at that time of year, they still get a lot of sunshine despite it being cold!

■ Investigate the culture.

When I was invited to work in Dubai, teaching foot reading to local people, I got myself a copy of "Culture Shock" for the area. (They do a whole series of books for different countries that give you an insight into the culture, the social etiquette and the business etiquette. I've always found them extremely useful so that you can avoid making any major mistakes and inadvertently upsetting your hosts.) I'd realised that when making my business proposal I would have to show an expense for a travelling companion – not because I needed one (I usually travel alone), but because in their culture it is unseemly for a woman to be unchaperoned, and would such an unchaperoned woman be deemed suitable to teach their daughters? Without one, I could have lost the opportunity. I also realised that my usual warm weather gear would not be appropriate because I'd have to cover my arms and legs. Luckily I have access to a personal shopper to whom I gave the criteria and who steered me towards the right outfits. Quite a few people told me that in Dubai it's much more westernised but because I was working with local people, I felt it more important to honour their culture and I was so glad that I did. We had a TV crew visit and on the day they visited all my students wore full abbaye so that only their eyes, feet and hands were showing. As it was, I stuck out anyway wearing bright colours compared to their black clothing. Imagine how ridiculous I would have felt in a less modest outfit.

■ Hire in the help you need.

Each time I work abroad, I know I can't do it all myself. I usually hire a PR and Marketing expert in that country to assist me. I'll need help even before I reach the country. They can advise me on the best approach to maximise my time there. They'll set up appointments with the relevant media, drip-feed them suitable articles prior to my arrival and build up a level of interest that we can convert into paying customers even before I arrive. They can advise me on suitable venues for my workshops and on pricing for the area. Sometimes, because of exchange rate differences, I'm able to ship over my books for sale (in which case I need an address and my "expert" who will be happy to keep them until I arrive). Sometimes the exchange rate will work against me, so I'll have to have some books printed in that country. I would need help with sourcing such a facility.

■ Don't underestimate how lonely you may feel.

I often stay a few months on my first trip to a country. This is so that I can spend some time building up my profile there through media interviews and offering talks and tasters prior to the actual teaching tour itself. It can be very lonely going back to an empty hotel room each night. Make sure you have a strategy to deal with this. I always have my laptop with me, so I upload some uplifting music and use it to set my mood. I also enjoy a good read, so if I'm away for a long time, then I borrow a gizmo on which I can download a bunch of e-books. It's much lighter than carrying a book and you can download a large number without impacting your airline weight restrictions! I read 20 e-books in Hawaii!

In America I contacted some local reflexologists and arranged to meet for a chat. We're still in touch now!

I go exploring my area in daylight so that at night I can safely go out for a dinner, avoiding the dodgy areas. It's much more fun to mingle with others than to sit alone in a hotel dining room and you're more likely to talk to other people if you pick a bustling restaurant that packs the tables in tight! Some nights I book to see a show or go exploring. Just because you're there to work doesn't mean you can't enjoy yourself. I also ask everyone I know if they know anyone in that area who I can meet up with. You'd be surprised just how many people will know someone they can suggest. Just knowing one person in an area can open up a whole new experience to you. One of my friends recently went to work abroad. Initially she found it tough being alone until (as she put it) "I thought, "What would Jane do?" So I took a leaf out of your book and treated it like I was going out on an adventure".

■ Tap into the existing communities. As a Reflexologist I can contact the reflexology associations in those countries to gain information, offer articles, pay for advertising to their membership and ask for help (if you don't ask, you don't get and what's the worst they can say? No?)

■ Calculate a budget. You won't know all the costs involved in your trip but you can prepare a budget and calculate whether you think the trip is worth making at all. Be realistic. For my first trip to Australia, we calculated the cost of

   ◆ International Flights

   ◆ Internal flights to each city on the tour

   ◆ Car or taxi hire

   ◆ Accommodation in each city (and managed to reduce this cost by staying with some very generous people who offered to put me up in their home – some who'd never even met me before I made the trip, although got to know me a little over email in the run-up to the trip.)

- ◆ Hire of conference rooms (usually in hotels so that things like refreshments could be provided with minimum hassle, projection screens would be available etc)
- ◆ Hire of equipment (we looked into the cost of hiring projectors but in the end I took my own laptop and projector to keep the costs down). I'd suggest if you are going to be doing a lot of travelling, invest in a very light and compact projector!
- ◆ Subsistence costs – well you've got to eat some time!
- ◆ Hire of expert help (PR and Marketing and a small budget for unforeseen expenditure such as designing a new ad etc)
- ◆ Cost of advertising for workshops
- ◆ Cost of book printing, binding and transporting to different destinations
- ◆ Cost of photocopying
- ◆ Cost of visa
- ◆ Cost of hiring someone to cover my business back home, checking and answering emails, fulfilling orders and fielding telephone calls

Once we'd worked out all those costs we had an idea of how much the tour would cost. Then we estimated how many attendees we'd need on each seminar in order to break even. Then we estimated how many attendees we'd need in order to make a reasonable profit.

- ■ Have an early bird discount. It's better that you have attendees signed up and paid before you get on that flight, than turn up in a country wondering if you're going to get any at all!
- ■ Consider whether you can create a multiple income stream during your trip.

On a recent trip, I was invited there primarily to give a workshop. However, my contact discussed with a therapy store whether she could hire a room there and set about arranging one-to-one foot readings at the store for me. She also set up a few private foot reading parties.

■ Consider how you are going to arrange and receive payments. It may be worth setting up a foreign currency account. Or you can submit foreign cheques to your normal account and arrange bank transfers from your normal account to a foreign account if you are willing to pay the bank charges accordingly. You'll need to investigate the charges. Sometimes it is more cost effective to cash a cheque in that country and bring home the foreign currency as cash to exchange. The advantage is that it's cheaper to exchange currency than to negotiate a foreign cheque. But the disadvantage is in carrying so much cash.

Risk

Risk

"Risk comes from not knowing what you are doing." Warren Buffett

I was reading a newspaper when I came across an article about a chap called Professor Spiegelhalter of the University of Cambridge. He was advocating the teaching of risk in schools. He said "We seem to grossly over-interpret immediate stories that happen to individuals around us, and from an evolutionary point of view, that may be enormously valuable. (It's better to run away from a predator, even if you're mistaken.) It's very difficult to think calmly about uncertainty. That's why it needs to be taught."

As I was reading it, I was thinking about my business and the risks I've taken over the years. I was thinking about that associated feeling every time I knew I was taking a risk. Then I recognised his use of the word uncertainty. That's exactly it in a nutshell. Risk is all about uncertainty of outcome. So if you are able to reduce the uncertainty over the outcome, you can minimise the risk. Simple!

So thinking about your business and the risks you are thinking of taking – how can you reduce the uncertainty?

- Investigate further. What statistics can you seek for your purpose? What information can you glean in order to improve your chances?
- Look at the overall pattern. Whilst you can't predict exactly how every precise event will happen, you can predict an overall pattern. (You don't know if your cat will like this cat food, but 8 out of 10 cats do, so you've got an 80% likelihood that it will.)
- Compare like with like.

- Ask yourself "What am I not being told?"

- Sleep on your decisions and discuss them with people who've had direct experience or expertise in the matter before making that decision.

- Think twice before acceping advice from people who have had no direct experience.

- When looking at percentages, remember that twice not very much is still not very much!

Calculating Risk – an example.

I've never been that hot with numbers. So when I have to look at numbers, I try to break them down into something more meaningful. Say to me that you have to spend £2,000 and I will feel an instinctive sense of panic because to me that sounds like a big number. Over the years, I've learned a way to get comfortable with dealing with such numbers and such a gut reaction. For example, if I'm considering producing a project that will cost me £2,000 to implement, I calculate how many items I would need to sell in order to recoup that investment.

£2,000 ÷ £50 = 40

So, if the item costs £50 then I would need 40 people to make a purchase in order to break even. I ask myself whether that is a feasible number. Then I ask myself how many people I could realistically expect to buy that item. That would tell me if the potential profit would be worth the investment. You'll hear people talk about R.O.I. They just mean the "return on investment". They want to know whether spending that much money as an investment will bring in enough profit to make it worthwhile.

If the bank is giving 5% interest as its savings rate, then £2,000 divided by 100 multiplied by 5 =£100 (5% interest)

That means I would need to sell two extra items at £50 (making a total of 42 items sold) in order to make the same return on investment as I would if I'd just left the money in the bank.

Selling over 42 items at £50 would mean I would start to make a profit and would be better off having taken the risk than leaving the money in the bank.

The part of this equation that you cannot quantify through money is all the fun you will have implementing the idea, the sense of achievement you will have if it succeeds and the background worry. "Will it work or won't it?"

Considering the above example, I'd also add that if you are going to start a new project, when you calculate the costs, allow an amount for failure. If you think you can sell 42 items, then set your pricing so that if you only sell 30 you'll still break even. In that way, you've got an extra safety factor.

Other ways of minimising the risk are

- Set up a limited liability company to handle the project so that if you do fail, the losses to yourself will be limited and you won't go completely bankrupt.
- Don't use personal money – if the company is liable then your personal funds, up to a point, are safe.
- Evaluate the risk to create a strategy
  - ◆ Consider the amount of risk that is acceptable to you
  - ◆ Identify and prioritise the risks
  - ◆ Understand the catalysts that could cause those risks to happen
  - ◆ Overcome your fear of risk by
    - ● Analysing financial and other data
    - ● Reviewing a successful business case
    - ● Learning from other business initiatives and projects
    - ● Undertake a SWOT analysis (strengths, weaknesses, opportunities and threats analysis as discussed earlier in this book)
    - ● Use scenario thinking. If x happens, then y…

Examples about asking people for advice:

When I wrote my first book, at a workshop the leader told me not to use a publisher. I challenged him after the workshop to ask if he really meant what he said. He told me that their experience of using a publishing house was that they lost the Rights to the work so if they wanted to bring out a video or a translated version then they couldn't do it without the permission of the publishing house. I didn't like the sound of that. He also told me that, despite their book being about making observations rather than making judgements, the editors decided to include a summary of conclusions at the end of each chapter – flying in the face of their whole philosophy.

Later, I found myself sitting next to a publisher at a dinner party. I asked her "If you had written your own book, would you self-publish or go through a publishing house?"
She replied "If I had the money and the marketing skills, I'd self-publish. If I didn't have the money I'd go to a publisher for the first one and self-publish the subsequent ones."

Tip: Before you take on board someone's advice, consider whether they have any first-hand knowledge or experience of what they are advising. It would be foolhardy to take a risk based on hearsay.

Top tips after
your first year

Top tips after your first year

Coach Paul Avins (www.paul-avins.com) gave the following tips

- Be a good boss to yourself. Do you allow yourself time off for holidays? Do you let yourself go home on time each night? Do you send yourself to bed when you get sick?

- Put on your investor's hat. Would you hire yourself? If you decide that the person I am being isn't doing it right, sack yourself, go outside the building, walk round it, come back in and rehire yourself if you've got back into the correct mindset.

- Building a business and selling it can be more profitable than running it.

- Look at your "blame list". Are you on it? Stop blaming others for what is not working. Stop making excuses.

- Break your big goals into smaller manageable ones.

- Create a marketing calendar to focus your attention on marketing each month despite your other commitments.

- Mix with people not in your industry to help spark new ideas.

- Once you have a successful business, systemise it and scale it up.

Greg Sheehan (my brother and chip shop/café owner) gave the following tips

- Make sure you are focused on doing only those things that will generate income. Pay someone else to do the non-income generating things and make sure you keep such costs to a minimum. Remember your time is much more valuable and you should remain focused on doing the important things.

- Employ a good lawyer and a good accountant right at the beginning.

- Join the Federation of Small Businesses.

My Tips

- Don't give up trying to sell yourself/your services. Every rejection you get is leading towards a "Yes". Keep going. Count the number of "No's" that lead to a "Yes" and then challenge yourself to beat the last record!

- Put a regular amount away each month in an ISA or similar to cover your tax bill.

- Leave your customers feeling happier when they leave you. Customer loyalty depends on a "feel-good" factor as well as good, reliable service.

- When giving suppliers instructions – do it in writing.

- Don't undervalue yourself.

- Be strict and disciplined with your time. Work time is work time. Play time is play time.

- Be as ruthless about scheduling fun time as you are about scheduling in business appointments.

- Don't try to do everything yourself.

- If it stops being fun for you, change it.

- Read *The E-Myth* by Michael Gerger. It's about why small businesses fail and how to avoid it.

I received an email from a fellow therapist when I was researching this book. I thought I'd include it here so that you can hear straight from someone who has launched their business and is juggling family and work commitments.

Thought this was an interesting topic for a book so am sending you my thoughts. Hope they help …

"I love the freedom of freelancing and the flexibility, working with people as equals.

I have a little 16 month old girl so working part time, I'm able to spend time with her & be a Mum, but it limited my ability to take bookings as I had little money for babysitting – so I was more reliant on my partner.

Now that she is older, I'm looking to take on another slot in a different centre, as the centre I have been working in has opened two new therapy rooms which has meant more clientele overall but also many new therapists, more competition & fewer bookings. I recognise that it could also be an opportunity to share & tap into our knowledge & experience as practitioners depending on how well we relate to each other - I realise that this challenging situation is always a chance for growth and evolution. Areas I need to improve are my promotional abilities, belief in my work as a therapist (I've been working for 6 years offering thai yoga massage) so now I'm looking at giving workshops (a great way to promote), build a website (long overdue), and specialise into areas of pregnancy massage & postnatal care.

I feel a bit wishy-washy as a therapist & not always on the ball to take opportunities and bookings that present themselves. I realise the need to keep training but also the fact that this requires money as does a new family …. the juggling act gets more difficult than when single …. more outgoings than incomings …. energy levels needing a boost. I know things get easier – I am happy to get down to my accounts in the evenings or when she is asleep during the day. Slowly I feel I'm getting there and my father, also a freelancer, often reminds me when to get my paperwork done.

My days are spent either at work three afternoons a week, organising baby & house, taking her to activities, shopping, library ... study in the evening is often difficult because usually I'm so tired ... but bit by bit I'll start to introduce it into my week & it will get easier again ... the juggling continues ... when I have no bookings at work I give promotional massages to staff/therapists/yoga teachers, do a yoga class, meditate & read ... its good "me time" and I really love it now - its so precious. (In the past, I used to worry more about the room rent being covered, making a profit etc.)

I find I'm always doing something ... the wheels keep turning ... the summer seems a difficult time in the freelance business, as does January and February. Most people go away - a good idea .... this year we couldn't and it feels like a very long summer ... but perhaps one whereby we're sorting out our systems & readjusting as a family unit ...

I think as long as you keep creative, working at new ideas in your business & your work as a therapist the energy keeps positive & flowing ... which keeps your business floating, making money and helping your growth.
Eve Khambatta
Thai Yoga Massage at www.thaitwists.co.uk

Independent advice

In the fourth year of running my business full time, I discovered that my local Business Link had introduced a scheme where their advisor would visit your business to discuss with you your progress.

They can offer some free advice or courses, help you see alternative solutions and act in a mentor-like role. I gather this is not available in all geographic locations but you may find they can point you to similar schemes.

At the end of our meeting, they produced a report which I then used to help me steer my business through the next steps.

Other friends have pooled resources and hired a "Wealth Coach". They meet once a month and are mentored through different business strategies. Somehow having a set time, set date to develop your strategy and having to report on progress is a great stimulus to action. It keeps you moving forward and often produces fresh ideas. I haven't joined them yet, but every time I meet those friends for coffee, I'm struck by how motivated they are and I often pick up tips and act on whatever they tell me they've been working on!

Employing staff

There are an estimated 3.7 million active businesses in the UK and over 2.3 million of these are businesses without employees. It's highly likely you won't initially be employing staff.

As your business grows, your needs will change and you may want to hire some help. So how do you find talented people, who are they and where do they hang out? And, when you find them, what do you need to know before you hire them?

In my business, I know that I can't do everything myself. For one, I haven't got all the skills necessary so I hire people who have the skills that I don't have, on a consultancy basis. By doing it this way, I avoid some of the many pitfalls of directly hiring staff. It may cost slightly more to hire a consultant rather than hiring a permanent staff member, but it means I can spread my budget over a range of skills as and when the projects require it, and if I find my budget is tight, I can choose not to hire in any skills for that period.

As I don't have direct experience of hiring staff, I went to a talk aimed at business owners given by Nicola Cameron and Clive Oliver of Peninsula (www.peninsula-uk.com, tel: 0800 542267) about employment law and health and safety. They kindly agreed to help me write this section. Do remember that the laws concerned may change and there are companies such as Peninsula who can oversee all this for you for a fixed fee.

Recruitment errors can be costly

A recent survey concluded that around 80% of CVs contain lies. Plus, once you hire someone (and even before you hire them) their rights are protected by employment laws. Knowing up front what this means to you as an employer will help you to be prepared. Adopting best practice will help to protect your business. Companies such as Peninsula can help you to set up procedures and keep up to date with changes in the law.

Finding the right people

How do you find the right people? You can use a recruitment consultant who can act as your HR Department. They will write the job description, prepare the advert, conduct the interviews and produce a short list of candidates for you. All of this you could, obviously, do yourself if you have the time, inclination and are a good judge of character.

Always request references and then speak to the referees. A lot can be conveyed in speech that would never be put to paper!

Adding value?

Employing an extra person may be 50% of your costs or 90% of your problems! Before employing them, ask yourself, will this extra person add value to my company?

There are ways that you can encourage them to be a team player. If you incentivise the individual through a commission structure, they may have an "I'm working for myself" attitude. But if you can set up a salary plus commission structure that is based on the team's performance you will be rewarding good team behaviour yet still encourage business growth.

Advertising in a local paper or at a local therapy school for help is a good place to start as most people are tied to a geographic location. Just be aware of indirect discrimination i.e. where you are advertising could exclude sectors of the workforce.

Employing family and friends may seem like a good idea, but if things don't work out, you may not just be losing an employee…

You'll need to
- Understand employee rights
- Create effective contracts
- Have access to up-to-date advice on changes to the law
- Have an awareness of common pitfalls
- A knowledge of how future regulations are progressing and how and when they may impact your business

There have been around 200 new acts since 1997 relating to employment law. If you breach procedures you can find yourself facing a claim. Ignorance may be bliss but it is not a defence.

Job applicants have rights. If you didn't give them the job, could you fight a claim that you didn't give them a job because they were of the wrong sex, colour, religion, or age?

Set up a standards and expectations manual so that, once you have hired someone, you can show them your high standards, and you then have a disciplinary route if one becomes necessary.

Keep job descriptions up to date.

There's currently a fixed penalty for failure to issue a contract of employment within 8 weeks of joining. It's best to issue the contract of employment immediately so that new employees know the rules straight away and understand what will happen if they break your rules.

Statutory disputes resolution procedure

Hopefully, once you've hired your new staff, your business will continue to grow and you'll all live happily ever after.

But if you're a realist, you'll want to know what the procedure is if things start to go wrong. The statutory disputes resolution procedure[3] (at time of going to print) is as follows:

■ Employees have a right to be accompanied at a disciplinary, grievance and appeal hearing. But by whom? A trade union official or a fellow employee. It's not usual to allow a relative as it would become too emotional. You can specify whom in the contract of employment.

■ Set down in writing the reason for the disciplinary hearing.

■ Hand a copy to the employee – get them to sign a receipt.

■ Ensure the employee has enough time to consider a response. Courts don't like less than 24 hours so make sure that you allow over 24 hours.

■ Hold a meeting with the employee so that they can discuss their response with you.

■ Conduct the meeting in a way that enables the employee to explain their position.

■ Consider your decision and after the meeting tell the employee of the decision.

3   Please check with your legal advisor what the latest advice is, as these laws are under review at time of going to print.

- Offer the employee a chance to appeal.
- Invite the employee to a meeting to discuss the appeal.
- Try to have a different person hold the appeal (a senior manager or another director who has not been involved in the initial disciplinary).
- The employee must invite a senior manager to the appeal meeting.
- Communicate the final decision to the employee (next stop is court).
- The timing of the meeting must be reasonable.
- The location of the meeting must be reasonable.
- You, the employer, must not delay unreasonably over any of the above steps.

Depending on what the employee has done, you may need to suspend the person until the procedure is carried out – make sure you give them full pay or you are assuming their guilt and courts will say you've already made your mind up.

OK – I know all this sounds heavy. I'm including the information in this book because recently someone I know was awarded a large sum of money because her employers did not follow the correct procedure when making her redundant. The reasons for the redundancy were legitimate but the correct legal procedure was not followed. As her friend, I was delighted for her. But as a business owner, I was horrified! At a time when the business needed to cut costs to survive, it had to pay out a large sum of money.

Potentially fair reasons for dismissal

At time of going to print acceptable reasons for dismissal[4] of an employee could be:

---

4   The law changes rapidly so please take legal advice to ensure you are up to date.

- Conduct (what constitutes good conduct?)
  - Poor time-keeping
  - Breaches of your sickness policy
  - Breaches of your dress code
  - Breach of Health and Safety rules
  - Gross misconduct

  Deal with conduct issues in a measured way. Ensure you have your defence in place first, through your contract of employment, your standards and procedures manuals, up-to-date job descriptions etc. Keep written records of the breaches and take advice on how to conduct the warnings.

- Capability
  - Performance
  - Long-term sick (take advice on the Disability Discrimination Act, the DDA)
  - Retirement
    - can't be less than 65 unless you are in an industry that allows this. If you retire an employee one day earlier than their 65th birthday then you could face a big payout – a recent case study of this cost the company £36,000.
  - Redundancy (you must have a solid business case for the redundancy – and take advice)
  - Statutory Ban
    - E.g. Have they got their driving licence?
  - Some other substantial reason (SOSR). (Must be substantial NOT convenient.)

Health and safety

Currently, if you employ less than five people you don't necessarily need to keep written evidence of your health and safety policy, procedures and risk assessments etc but you still have a duty of care and by law you must still have all these things in place – it's just not necessary to have them written down. (As all companies must comply and the only way you can prove that you do is by having it written down, this law is up for review and may be tightened.[5]) You are responsible for employees' health, safety and welfare and they are protected by law whilst at work.

Give them information, instruction, training and procedures. You must appoint a responsible person and a competent person – in small businesses this person may be one and the same but the onus is on "competent". Make a note of the responsible person on your Health and Safety Law poster (usually a director).

- Assess risk
- Implement measures identified as being necessary
- If an employee is pregnant then they need specific risk assessment
- If employing migrant workers
  - Ensure they understand the training given
- Consider sickness, protective equipment and training

If you supply protective equipment and it is not used and you don't point it out to your employees then you are potentially still liable.

Corporate manslaughter will mean an automatic police investigation in the event of a death on your premises.

---

5   The law changes rapidly. Please take legal advice to ensure you are up-to-date.

Have in place

- Fire Procedures
- Accident reporting
- Health and Safety Policy
- Training
- Process of Constant Review

You have a responsibility not just for you and your employees, but also your visitors and your contractors. You need to ensure that you have contracts, policies, procedures and documentation in place that covers them too.

Some of the areas you may need to create policies for

- Smoking
- Health and safety
- Harassment
- Internet usage
- Equal Opportunities
- Holidays
- Bullying
- Drugs
- Mobiles

- Email
- Sickness
- Hygiene
- Right to search
- Other employment
- Notice Period
- Mail
- Media
- Wastage
- Lone worker

- Stress
- Dress code
- Swearing
- Car
- Mobility
- Lay off
- Expenses
- Environment/ Sustainability

Again, if you find all this daunting, you can for a fixed fee find a company who will assist you with setting up your staff contracts and handbooks, health and safety policies and risk assessments, procedures, record keeping and monitoring etc. To contact the people who helped me with this chapter, you can visit www. peninsula-uk.com or contact Nicola directly on nicola.cameron@ peninsula-uk.com or 07772 320501.